PATHWAYS

Guidance Activities for Young Children

Leon H. Burton
Susan N. Woltag
University of Hawaii

▲▼ **Addison-Wesley Publishing Company**

Menlo Park, California • Reading, Massachusetts
Wokingham, Berkshire UK • Amsterdam • Don Mills, Ontario • Sydney

Acknowledgment

Grateful acknowledgment is made to the many teachers and children
who contributed to this book. Special thanks to Doris Fukumoto, Dan
Hazlett, and Carolyn Williams at the O'Connor Hospital Children's
Center, San Jose, California, Terry Shue, Director, and to Debbie
Nunn at the Sunnyvale Presbyterian Preschool, Sunnyvale, California,
Joyce Oglesbee, Director.

Book design by Betsy Bruneau-Jones.

This book is published by the Addison-Wesley INNOVATIVE DIVISION.

ISBN 0-201-20272-7
BCDEFGHIJKL-AL-89876

Contents

CHAPTER 4   *Relationships with Others Activities (Respect for Differences in Others)*

CHAPTER 5   *Physical and Emotional Growth Activities*

CHAPTER 6   *Decision-Making and Problem-Solving Activities*

CHAPTER 7   *Values of Learning Activities*

CHAPTER 8   *Awareness of the World of Work Activities*

Appendix

CHAPTER 1

Introduction

Young children are socially aware. They have the built-in motivation to grow and learn; to reach out and encounter; to react and interact; to search out of their experience those elements that give meaning, order, substance, and value to their lives.

Even very young children have intelligible speech. They smile. They interact with others. Their natural inquisitiveness excites them to seek out challenging activities. Moreover, they have begun to learn standards and prohibitions, rules and procedures. Their imaginative play both mirrors and transforms the adult activities that occur around them. As they grow, so does their sense of self, their capacity to share, their ability to work in groups and make decisions. As they grow, so does their ability to relate to others, their awareness of change and growth, their values, and their view of the world in which they live.

The child's early years greatly influence later social and emotional development, and early childhood educational programs play an increasing role in this process. So this book. The activities cover areas of guidance appropriate to early school experiences. They are not intended to replace on-the-spot learning occasions that occur every day. But the activities provide opportunities for interaction and practice that the teacher can draw upon to help children understand their special and unique characteristics and become fulfilled individuals.

General Categories of Guidance Activities

Six general categories of guidance activities have been selected for this book: Self-Awareness and Understanding, Relationships with Others, Physical and Emotional Growth, Decision Making and Problem Solving, Values of Learning, and Awareness of the World of Work. These categories subsume a host of guidance topics appropriate for and important to young children everywhere, and they are consistent with many state educational system plans for guidance and career education. No attempt has been made to include all possible topics for each category because of the voluminous set of materials such an approach would require. Those topics selected will, we believe, prove to be the most beneficial to children and teachers and make positive contributions to children's emotional, intellectual, physical, social, and aesthetic development.

The organization of topics by category is arbitrary. For instance, activities in all six categories will ultimately contribute to the development of self-awareness and understanding. Also, as children develop a positive self-concept this will influence directly their ability to relate socially with others. You are encouraged to accept these six closely related and overlapping categories only as an organizational scheme to identify primary emphases of the activities. The overlapping characteristics of the activities will soon become obvious to users of the book. (See the Index of Behaviors in the appendix.)

SELF-AWARENESS AND UNDERSTANDING

Young children need to develop positive self-concepts. Fifteen of the book's activities address this need. The following topics were used as bases for designing the activities.

Identifying feelings about self.

Learning to recognize personal characteristics others feel good about.

Becoming aware of physical abilities, social skills, and learning skills.

Becoming aware of personal behaviors that need to be changed.

Identifying personal interests in activities that involve family and friends.

Developing behaviors that demostrate respect for self and others.

Helping others to develop positive self-concepts.

Becoming aware of ways people are alike and different.

Learning social behaviors that encourage acceptance by others.

RELATIONSHIPS WITH OTHERS

Important in the life of every young child is the development of understandings and skills that contribute to successful relationships with others. Thirty-one activities address this need. Nine of the thirty-one are concerned specifically with learning to recognize and respect the differences we see in others. The following topics were used to design the activities.

Understanding the roles of family members.

Recognizing a need for cooperation and order in group activities.

Understanding the value of good communication skills.

Developing a respect for authority; recognizing the need for rules.

Learning to listen to others; accepting opinions of others.

Accepting ways people are alike and different (including age, sex, race, size, culture, handicapping conditions, etc.).

PHYSICAL AND EMOTIONAL GROWTH

Children need to recognize at a very early age the value of good physical and emotional health. This need is addressed by twenty-four of the activities. The following topics were used to design these activities.

Knowing the value of good personal health.

Becoming aware of problems associated with "growing up" and changing physical abilities.

Learning to recognize emotions and ways they are expressed.

Becoming aware that people make judgments about others based on the attitudes and behaviors they observe.

Becoming aware of acceptable and unacceptable ways of expressing emotions.

Identifying things that cause stress.

Becoming aware that emotions and stress influence behavior.

Exploring acceptable ways to cope with stress.

Understanding the reality of death.

DECISION MAKING AND PROBLEM SOLVING

Every person spends a lifetime dealing with problems and making decisions. So it is of utmost importance that children begin developing decision-making and problem-solving skills in their early years. This need is addressed by seven activities, which are based on the following topics.

Identifying problems.

Becoming aware of sources of helpful information.

Identifying alternative solutions to problems.

Basing decisions on valid information; checking the reliability of conclusions.

VALUES OF LEARNING

Eleven of the activities are concerned with developing an understanding of the value of learning. The following topics were used to design these activities. These meet the need young children have for understanding why learning is important and the role of the school, home, and community in meeting this need.

Recognizing the need for good use of time.

Learning to do tasks, seeking help when needed.

Developing good work habits.

Understanding the value of learning and schooling.

Awareness of the World of Work

Every person spends the most years of his or her life in a "worker" role. There is a need for young children to develop an awareness of the world of work and how learning and personal development relate to what a person will do in the adult years. Twelve of the activities meet this need by addressing the following topics.

Exploring the world of work; understanding why certain occupations interest some people.

Identifying a wide range of occupations.

Understanding how learning prepares people for work.

Recognizing home, school, and community activities in which people participate.

Learning to work cooperatively in a group.

Contributing to group tasks by accepting responsibilities.

The Activities

This book has 100 activities that may be used in any sequence. All are intended for groups of children, but many could be adapted for individual experience. The activities are listed in the Contents by title and page number.

FORMAT OF THE ACTIVITIES

A single format is used for all 100 activities. Each has a title that relates to the area of guidance selected for emphasis. Beneath each title is a brief description of the primary behavior children are expected to develop, at least in part, as a result of participation in the activity.

The next section, "Materials," lists all items needed to conduct the activity. Art supplies, props, pictures, furniture, musical instruments, assorted objects, tools, sound sources, etc., are listed. Items needed for extension activities are not included in the list.

The "Activity" section briefly summarizes the procedures and intended outcomes of experience.

The main section of the activity is titled "Procedures." These are step-by-step instructions for beginning the activity and guiding it to completion. You may elect to personalize the procedures after you become familiar with the activity plan. Many activities can be adapted to accommodate your children's and your own interests and abilities. The procedures do not provide a complete dialogue appropriate for all children in all situations. Therefore, you must improvise a dialogue when needed to maintain an interesting flow of events. Your improvised dialogue should always lead children to the discovery of important guidance principles rather than provide specific answers without stimulating thought about personal and social development. We urge you to keep this in mind as you adapt the procedures and improvise dialogue.

"Extension Activity" is the next section; it describes follow-up procedures that build upon the children's skills and understandings developed earlier. The purpose here is to provide reinforcement if interest is high and time available.

Photographs are included to show children participating in one or more of the procedures described in the activity.

Level of Difficulty of the Activities

Some of the activities are more difficult than others. A wide range has been included to accommodate the needs and interests of (1) children who are older or progressing faster than others and (2) children who are younger or need repeated experiences and reinforcement.

Several activities are especially designed for older and more experienced children; however, parts of these could be completed by younger or less experienced children. The following are examples of ways you could adapt parts of activities you believe are too difficult for the children in your group.

I Can Do It Too! (Chapter 2, p. 18) Should younger children be unable to copy simple drawings, you could have them copy simple body movements such as hand claps, head pats, drawing circles with elbows, tummy rubs, hopping, knee bends, etc. Let them describe in their own words how their movements looked like or looked different from yours.

Self-Assessment Game (Chapter 2, p. 24) Children who do not read will be unable to respond by circling "yes" or "no." You could adapt the activity by asking them, one by one, to respond verbally, circling answers for them that you will record and later file for future reference.

Helpers (Chapter 3, p. 50) A child may not be able to recreate his or her family through the collage procedure. An older child could assist by asking the younger child to name each person living in the home, then helping to select and cut out pictures to represent them and create the collage.

We All Need to Help Each Other (Chapter 4, p. 88) Some children may not want to be blindfolded. A child who resists could hold one hand of a blindfolded child as you hold the other hand. The three of you then go for a walk. During the walk you could talk with the blindfolded child about how he or she feels so the reticent child will have a first-hand experience with the activity.

Stop and Go Decisions (Chapter 6, p. 168) Younger children who are unable to conceptualize the relationship of a traffic light's colors to appropriate times for movement could be paired with an older child. Ask the older child to lead the younger child across the intersection, explaining why he or she is waiting, looking, moving, etc.

Places We Learn (Chapter 7, p. 192) The use of "side coaching" for younger children will be helpful with this activity (and with many others in this book). A child may select a picture but not be able to identify what he or she could learn from the place pictured. Use of questions keyed to the main features of the picture will stimulate thought and help a younger child recognize something previously not seen.

Activities can often be adapted for younger and less experienced children by reducing the number of operations required and having them deal with one thing at a time. Pairing an older child with a younger or less experienced child can also be valuable in adapting activities. The older child, in some instances, will be better able to verbalize aspects of an activity, using terminology that will stimulate a quick response by the younger child. Users of this book will seek viable ways to involve in some way very young children in all of the activities.

The Teacher's Homework

It is important that you read and reflect on all the introduction material carefully before beginning the activities. Scan the contents pages, familiarize yourself with the activities and their format, and become acquainted with the material in the appendix. You might then study many activities before selecting those for the children's earliest experiences.

Before getting the activities underway, be certain that you have become thoroughly familiar with the six guidance topics selected for emphasis in this book. A good knowledge and understanding of these topics will help you relate one experience to another, using an activity to extend the experience gained from activities presented earlier.

You will find it helpful to prepare and maintain cumulative folders for each child as you select and design activities. Entering brief comments in the folders on how well each child was able to follow the procedure — and the general interest shown in the activity — will help you plan future experiences. Be certain to record which activities the children as a whole have completed. Those completed by all children that generated high interest should be repeated periodically to provide opportunities for further refining skills and expanding understanding.

For how many activities must you prepare materials to get underway? It depends on how quickly you want to use the activities. Some teachers prepare materials for only one or two activities at a time; others prepare for many so they will have a wider selection to accommodate the children's varied interests. Whichever approach you use, prepare the materials to withstand repeated use. You will need adequate storage areas and a simple identification system for materials. Masters for several activities are included in the appendix. These may be duplicated and used in any way to help meet your instructional needs.

Use of This Book with Other Curriculum Materials

This book is intended for use with other curriculum materials and with the activities you and others have designed. It is suggested that you review all materials and teacher-designed activities you currently use, then decide how this book's activities could best be woven into your teaching plans. Another approach is to use the activities at appropriate times during the year when they relate in a direct way to the children's personal and interpersonal development needs. Use of the activities to meet specific needs of the children and your ongoing counseling of individual children together will form a comprehensive guidance program in your school. It is the intent of the authors that the activities will help young children better understand themselves and become successful in their relationships with others and the world in which they live.

CHAPTER 2

Self-Awareness and Understanding Activities

Alike, But Different

The children will develop an awareness of ways they are alike and ways they are different from each other.

Materials

- Three four-legged chairs of different size and color (or three other similar objects or pieces of furniture)
- String, scissors, paper, and felt-tip pens for tracing

Activity

The children first identify similarities and differences among three chairs of different size and color. They then identify ways the chairs are alike and ways they are different.

Procedures

Show the three chairs to the children and help them identify ways the chairs are similar and different. Their observations might include the following.

Similarities	*Differences*
four legs	color
seat with back	size (big, medium, small)
used for sitting (sometimes standing)	design
all three are chairs	specific lengths (legs, backs)
found in homes and schools	normally used by people of different sizes

Select three children who differ in size to stand before the other children. You might ask questions such as the following to help focus their perceptions on similarities and differences.

Are all three girls? (boys)

What body parts do all three have?

Are their arms the same length? (Cut lengths of string for each child's arm length to show differences.)

Can all three talk, walk, run, sing, cut paper with scissors?

Do all three need to eat and sleep?

Which of the three need to brush their teeth?

Are their feet, hands, and heads the same size? (Traced, cut-out hand and feet patterns could be compared.)

Which of the three have the same (or different) hair color?

Use the above questions and others to help the children learn to recognize their own unique characteristics as well as their sameness.

Extension Activity

Organize the children in pairs and have them each tell how they are alike and different from their partners. The partners also could describe things they like and do not like to do; this will help them identify similarities and individual uniqueness.

My Interests, Ours, and Theirs

The children will learn to identify their own interests and those of others.

Activity

The children learn to identify a wide range of personal interests and the interests they share with others. They also identify interests of others that they do not share.

Procedures

Ask the children to name some of their favorite places they like to go (park, beach, amusement park, shopping center, store, church, party, movie, etc.). Keep a record of each child's favorite place or places as they name them. After the list is complete, point out which children named a certain place. Help them build an understanding that some places they like to go are not the same as all the other children's. Emphasize the understanding that we each rightfully have personal interests that may not be shared by others.

Follow this same procedure to point out differences in interests such as foods, games, TV shows, craft activities, etc.

Extension Activities

Identify an activity (such as taking a walk to look at flowers, picking up refuse around the school area, arranging equipment and other objects in a nice order, etc.) that the children say they have little interest in, and initiate procedures to try to gradually change their interest in a positive way. The goal is to help them learn that their interests can change over a period of time.

Improving My Abilities

The children will learn to compete with themselves to improve their individual abilities.

Materials

- 3″ × 5″ cards for teacher to keep permanent record of each child's progress
- Chalk, masking tape, or string

Activity

The children demonstrate and then practice to improve their abilities in several areas. Their progress is recorded over a period of time. The children learn the importance of competing with themselves to improve their individual abilities.

Procedures

Explain to the children that you are going to help them learn about their abilities in several areas. Use chalk, masking tape, or string to mark off a line where the children will stand and one-by-one jump the greatest distance they can. A measurement is made for each child to where his or her heels landed on the surface. Record on the cards the distances they were able to jump and the date. After the initial jump, the children should periodically practice to improve their jumping abilities. Measurements can be made again every two months and recorded on the cards to show the progress children have made over a period of time. Follow a similar procedure to record the times elapsed for stacking twenty books one on top of the other, running a distance marked off on the playground, etc. The purpose is to involve the children in competing against themselves to improve their abilities, not to compete with the other children. Point out that all children should work to improve their abilities in several areas and that the activities in school help them to do this.

Extension Activity

Identify other abilities that will require the children to compete with themselves, such as lining up alphabet cards in the correct order, lining up number cards in their numerical order, reciting from memory days of the week and months of the year, etc. As different abilities are developed, a note to parents indicating for example that "Susan has developed the ability to. . ." may be useful in impressing on the children the fun and excitement they can have developing new abilities.

This Is My Face

The children will learn to identify and accept their physical characteristics.

Activity

The children will identify the features of their faces through the sense of touch and accept their faces as special and unique.

Procedures

Seat the children so they can see you. Gently touch various parts of your face, describing your actions in a little chant. For example:

> I'm touching my head.
>
> I'm feeling my hair.
>
> I'm tugging my ears.
>
> I'm touching my face.
>
> I'm tapping my nose.
>
> I'm covering my mouth.
>
> I'm touching my lips.

Tell the children it is now their turn to explore their special faces. Guide them with simple instructions as they explore their faces. For example:

> Put your hands on your head and feel it. Is it hard? soft? Feel the bumpy spots. Feel how it is shaped.
>
> Now stroke your hair. How does it feel? (smooth, crinkly, wispy, etc.)
>
> Now touch your ears on the outside only. Feel your earlobes.
>
> Now close your eyes and run your fingers gently over your face. Find the soft spots. Find the hard spots.
>
> Touch your nose with your finger. Is it fuzzy like a bunny rabbit or smooth like a puppy?
>
> Now touch your eyebrows. Can you feel the bone underneath?
>
> Move your fingers over your lips. Do they feel different from the rest of your face?

Stop the exploring activity before children lose interest. Tell them their faces are special, making the point that no two people have faces that feel exactly alike.

Extension Activity

Use the same procedure to help children explore the muscles and bones of their hands, arms, feet, and legs. Call their attention to the soft parts, the hard parts, and the parts that bend and move.

I Can Do It Too!

The children will interact with one another and imitate the patterns created by others.

Materials

- 8½″ × 11″ paper divided into four sections (one sheet for every two children)
- Crayons or felt-tip pens

Activity

The children pair off and play a game in which a drawing by one child serves as a model for a drawing by a second child. The roles are then reversed, with the second child's drawing serving as a model for the first. The children discuss similarities and differences in their drawings. They learn that imitating what others do is one way to learn things.

Procedures

Demonstrate what "copying" is by asking one child to draw something simple then by your copying what was drawn. Show the children the two drawings and explain what you did.

Have the children pair off. Give each pair a sheet of paper divided into four sections. Ask the first child to draw something in one square; have the second child copy it in the adjacent square. Reverse the roles and have the second child serve as a model for the first.

Ask the children to discuss with each other the similarities and differences in their drawings. Point out that we learn to do many things by watching what others do and imitating them.

Extension Activity

Vary the original activity by having children copy body movements; puppet movements; designs made with blocks, beads, or tiles; songs; etc.

I Have Feelings Too!

The children will learn that they have feelings and that these are natural and okay.

Materials

One or more of the following books: *Nobody Asked Me If I Wanted a Babysitter*, Martha Alexander (New York: Dial Press, 1971); *We Never Get to Do Anything*, Martha Alexander (New York: Dial Press, 1971); *Will I Have a Friend?*, Miriam Cohen (New York: MacMillan, 1967); *Staying Home Alone on a Rainy Day*, Chihiro Iwasako (New York: McGraw-Hill, 1969); *Whistle for Willie*, Ezra Jack Keats (New York: Viking Press, 1964); *Alexander and the Terrible, Horrible, No Good, Very Bad Day*, Judith Viorst (New York: Atheneum, 1972); *Where the Wild Things Are*, Maurice Sendak (New York: Harper & Row, 1963).

Activity

The children talk about their feelings and experience them in pantomimes. They express their feelings about recent school happenings that the teacher calls to their attention. They then listen to a story about a child who has feelings like theirs.

Procedures

Before reading, talk with the children about feelings such as anger, sadness, loneliness, aggression, and so forth. Illustrate one or more of these in a brief pantomime. Describe one or two specific situations that recently happened to the children in school. Ask the children involved to act out how they felt. For example, "How did you feel, John, when you broke your cup?"

Select one of the books from the list above that is in keeping with what the children express. Read it to the group. As you read, elicit from the children what feelings are involved at various points in the story. For example: "When Max in *Where the Wild Things Are* is sent to his room without eating anything, how does he feel?"

When you finish, ask the children to recollect similar experiences.

Extension Activity

Have children paint "feeling pictures": happy, sad, angry, bored, jealous. Ask them what feelings their drawings represent. Label the pictures and display them.

The Five Senses

The children will learn to identify and to develop a better awareness of the five senses.

Materials

- Rhythm instruments: rhythm sticks, maracas, jingle clogs, tone block, drum, etc.
- Three objects to be felt: smooth sheet of hard plastic, sandpaper block, furry toy
- Slice of apple, section of orange, slice of banana, slice of pear
- Raisins, small pieces of apple, small pieces of bread, dry-roasted (shelled) peanuts, small pieces of carrot (or substitutes)
- Paper or plastic dishes for food items

Procedures

Pick out an interesting object in the room and direct the childrens' attention to it. Ask them to look closely and then describe the characteristics of the object they see. Help them understand that they can describe what they see because of their sense of sight.

Select five rhythm instruments, show and identify them for the children, then play each for a few seconds. Help them learn to associate the sound of the instruments with their names. Then stand behind the children, play one of the instruments, and ask the children to name the instrument you played (they should not peek). When they can name each instrument by its sound, point out that hearing also is one of the senses we enjoy.

Have all the children close their eyes, or use blindfolds for some or all of the children. Ask them to take turns feeling three objects and identifying each as smooth, furry, or rough. Help them develop an awareness of touch as another important sense through which we can recognize and enjoy things.

Again have all the children close their eyes, or use blindfolds for some or all of the children. They are to take turns smelling four different kinds of fruit and identifying each by its odor. Another sense they should become more aware of is smell.

All children should close their eyes, or some or all should wear blindfolds. Place one of each of the small pieces of food on a plate. Help them reach, find, and then eat each of the items. They are to identify each item after eating it. Point out that the sense of taste makes it possible for them to identify what they are eating.

Review with the children each of the five senses and how they are important to so many aspects of their lives.

Extension Activity

Select one of the senses (such as hearing) and organize a game. Ask half the children to find objects that make sounds. As the objects are found, they should be hidden in a box and not be shown to the other children. Those children who found the objects should produce (one at a time) a sound using the objects. The goal is for the children listening to guess what object is making the sound. The game is intended to increase children's sensory awareness of sound. Similar games could be organized to increase awareness of the other senses.

"Self-Assessment" Game

The children will learn the value of self-assessment to improve the school environment.

Materials

- Large sheet of poster paper (or other paper)
- Response sheet for each child

Activity

The children identify things that contribute to having fun during group activities. A list is compiled and written on poster paper for future use. The items are later read, and the children use response sheets to rate themselves for each of the items. The procedure is repeated periodically to encourage self-assessment.

Procedures

Ask the children to name some things that make it fun to be with other children in the class (having room to play, having a chance to share materials, getting along without arguments, having a friend who helps, etc.). Compile a list of the things they name; use prompter questions such as the following only as needed to stimulate thought.

Do we:
Help people when they need help?
Help to keep our room clean?
Share with others?
Take turns and give everyone a chance?
Run and bump into others when we are supposed to be walking?
Give mean looks to others instead of smiles?
Follow the teacher's instructions?
Bother others when they are in our way?
Say "excuse me," "I am sorry," etc., when we unintentionally disturb others?

When the list is complete, write — using as few words as possible — on poster paper the things named. Near the end of the school day ask the children to rate themselves for each of the things they named. A response sheet like the following should be prepared for each child.

Name	
1. YES	NO
2. YES	NO
3. YES	NO
4. YES	NO
etc.	

As you read each item and its corresponding number, ask the children to circle "yes" or "no" to indicate whether they believe they did things to make school fun for the other children in the group. Encourage the idea of making an honest self-assessment for the purpose of improvement and contributing to the good of all. Periodically during the year have the children assess themselves again using the same items they named. Revise the list when needed.

Extension Activity

Have the children name things that make playground time more fun for everybody. When a list is compiled, use the list and response sheets following a playground experience to have the children assess themselves. Encourage honest self-assessment as a way to make playground time more fun for everyone.

My Name Has a Special Sound

The children will learn that their names have unique rhythms.

Materials

- Drum and mallet

Activity

The children learn to identify their name rhythms and move in time to the beat. They discover the uniqueness of their name rhythms and that they share name rhythms with others.

Procedures

Play the rhythm of each child's first name, saying the name as you play. Vary loudness and length to achieve individuality. For example, Kimmie and Bobby have a long-short (dum-ta) rhythm, Suzanne has a short-long rhythm (ta-dum), Roberta has a short-long-short (ta-dum -ta) rhythm, and Jonathan a long-short-short (dum-ta-ta) rhythm.

Tell the children that when they hear their name rhythms they should stand. You might begin with two-syllable names that sound short-long, such as Marie, Jeanette, Armand. When these children identify themselves, play the name rhythms over and over and invite them to move in tempo while saying their names to the beat. Repeat the procedure with two-syllable names that are long-short, one-syllable names, and three-syllable names (long-short-long, short-short-long, etc.), and so forth.

For children whose names have uncommon patterns, point out the uniqueness of their name rhythms. You might also tell these children that others share their name rhythms. For children with more common patterns, indicate that they share name rhythms with many others.

Extension Activity

Include the children's last names when you feel they are ready. Each child can then do his or her own name dance.

My Voice Has a Special Sound Game

The children will learn to recognize that everyone's voice is special and has a unique sound.

Activity

The children discuss how people's voices differ from one another. They then play a voice identification game in which they guess the identity of their classmates by the voices they hear.

Procedures

Ask the children whether they can tell their mother's voice from their father's voice, even with their eyes closed. When they say "yes," explain that each has a voice that is special. Voices are different just like faces are different.

Gather the children in an open area of the classroom. The child who is "It" crouches in the center and hides his or her face while the others scatter around the room. At the teacher's signal, one of the children calls "Come here" while the others remain silent. By remembering the sound of the voice and where it came from, the child who is "It" tries to guess the identity of the person who called. If necessary, you can ask the caller to repeat the phrase.

Extension Activity

Tape record the voices of each child in your group. Play the recording, pausing after each voice, while the children try to identify the speaker.

Names for Body Parts Game

The children will learn the names of the parts of their bodies.

Materials

- One beanbag for each child

Activity

The children learn the terms for parts of their bodies by playing a simple game. Following your instructions, they place beanbags on parts of their bodies. Later, they attempt the leader's role, telling others where to place the beanbags.

Procedures

Have the children put the beanbags on different parts of their bodies, following your verbal instructions. Start with things they can do while standing:

Put the beanbag on top of your head.
Put it on your right shoulder; left shoulder.
Hold it in your hand.
Put it on the palm of your hand.
Balance it on your fingers.
Put it on your knee.

Next, name things they can do sitting and/or lying down:

Put the beanbag on your stomach.
Put it on your chest.
Place it on your right leg; left leg.
Balance it on your nose.

Finally, have them pair up and take turns placing the beanbag on their partners' bodies:

Put it in the middle of the back.
Put it on the buttocks.
Put it on the upper back.

You might want to ask volunteers to give instructions. Help them name the body parts should they forget the proper terms. Guide them to see that there are ways to describe most areas of the body.

Extension Activity

Play a "Simon Says" game, using body parts in each command. For example, you might say, "Simon says touch your nose. Touch your stomach. Simon says rub your stomach."

Finger Puppet Family

The children will become sensitive to the actions and feelings of family members in different situations.

Materials

- Precut, oval-shaped pieces of paper (approximately 1″ × 1½″)
- Felt-tip pens
- Two-way tape

Activity

The children practice creating finger puppet faces. After being given a family situation, they select roles and create dialogues. With guidance they identify the feelings involved, drawing faces that express those feelings.

Procedures

(Children should first have completed "Finger Puppet Talk," p. 116, before beginning this activity.)

Invite them to practice drawing faces on the oval-shaped pieces of paper. Encourage them to experiment with different expressions (happy, sad, angry, etc.).

Pair the children. Present them with a family "situation" involving two family members. The situation should be specific enough for the children to generate a dialogue between the characters. For example:

> You don't like boiled carrots, but your daddy puts them on your plate.
>
> Your mommy is going shopping. You want to go but she wants you to stay at home.
>
> Your brother gets a new toy. You want to play with it.

Invite the children to each select a role and draw a face expressing the feeling in that situation. You might have to help them identify the feeling they want to portray. Attach each completed face to the children's index fingers with two-way tape.

The children should then improvise a dialogue to match the situation while they assume the role of the family member whose face they have drawn. Have them explain why they feel as they do. You might use prompter questions to help them verbalize: "How does the mommy feel? What does she say?"

The purpose is to explore family interactions and how people's actions affect the feelings of others. The following is a list of situations children might explore.

> Requesting to do chores.
> Going to bed.
> Brushing teeth.
> Eating a disliked meal.
> Getting up in the morning.
> Saying goodbye when parents go out.
> Being left out of a family activity.
> Greeting a visiting relative.

Extension Activity

The children can create finger puppet families using fabric, yarn, etc. Groups of three or four children can explore family situations involving more than two members.

If You Try It You Might Like It

The children will learn that their dislikes for some foods may be only imagined rather than a result of experience.

Materials

- Small pieces or slices of several raw vegetables that you believe most of the children will not like (pickles, celery, cucumbers, lettuce, cauliflower, etc.)
- Tray for foods

Activity

The children identify favorite foods and foods they do not like. They then explain why they do not like to eat certain foods, whether their dislike is imagined or real. Small pieces or slices of food that most of the children will probably not like are then made available to them for trial purposes. An attitude of openness toward eating new foods is encouraged.

Procedures

Invite the children to name some of their favorite foods, then some they do not like to eat. Ask them to explain why they do not like to eat certain foods. Try to get specific answers such as taste, appearance, smell, texture, color, etc. For the foods they identify that they do not like to eat, ask whether they have actually eaten the foods or whether upon seeing or hearing about the foods they decided they did not want to eat them. It is important to help the children learn to recognize that sometimes we let our imaginations control decisions about eating certain foods and that what we think may be true about the taste of some foods is not true in actuality.

Invite the children to try some of the foods you have prepared. Name each of the foods on the tray. Then begin with one food, such as pickles. Determine which students like or do not like pickles. Have children who like pickles (if any) eat pickle slices and explain why they like them. Then encourage those who say they do not like pickles to eat a small piece on a trial basis. Follow the same or a similar procedure with the other foods you have prepared. The goal is not to use persistent persuasion to get the children to try eating new foods but rather to encourage openness and experimentation to learn whether what they have imagined is in fact true.

Extension Activity

Challenge the children to learn to eat one new food each week or month, whichever might be appropriate. When they have learned to eat new foods, have them tell the other children about the experience and why they think they will or will not be eating new foods in the future.

Comparing Colors

The children will learn both the uniqueness of their own skin colors and the range and variety of possible shades of skin.

Activity

The children compare skin colors and discover the great range and variety of skin shades.

Procedures

It is a truism that prejudice, although not innate in children, can be learned from the attitudes of parents and society. The teacher's attitude toward racial differences can be extremely important in creating harmony in a racially mixed class and in helping children accept the differences among themselves. Naturally, you will handle individual instances of racial prejudice as they occur. This activity is one that may be used on the spot when the issue of racial differences comes up during the day.

Have the children hold their bare arms next to one another. Point out the range of skin tones (olive, black, white, pinkish, brown, light brown, yellow, reddish). Use words the children will understand to call attention to the shades: honey-colored, creamy, soft pink, soft brown, etc. Be sure to point out the wide range of skin tones among members of one racial group. People labeled "white" range in color from dark olive to fair. Avoid racial labels, and concentrate on helping the children become aware of both their own uniqueness and the great variety of which they are a part.

Extension Activity

Make up puzzles by pasting magazine pictures of different-colored human faces on cardboard and cutting them into puzzle pieces. You might try mixing two of the puzzles, then pairing children to work the two puzzles together. When they finish, discuss how they were able to tell the faces apart.

Describing Our Friends

The children learn that individuals are distinguished by unique physical attributes and qualities.

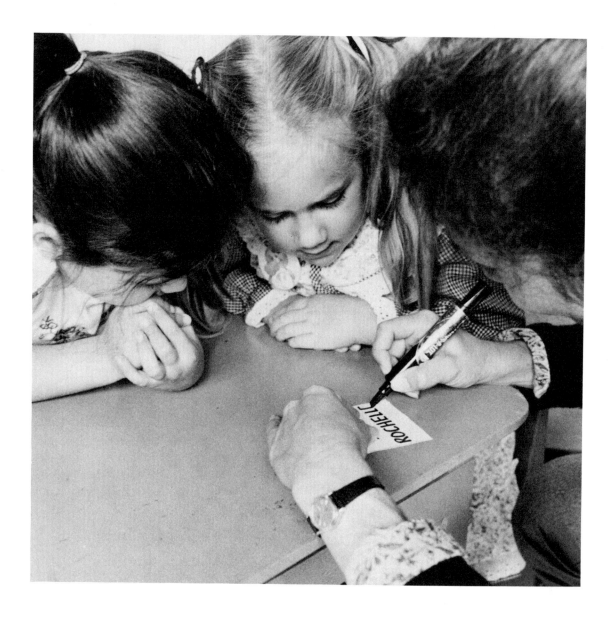

Materials

- Blank stick-on name tags
- Felt-tip pens

Activity

The children refine their descriptive vocabularies by describing the physical attributes and personal qualities of others. They learn that there are many words they can use besides names to distinguish one person from another.

Procedures

Tell the children that everyone is given a name when he or she is born. Discuss how a name is a *label*, a word used to tell one person from another. Say that you will show them what a name can do, then call one child by name, saying, for example, "Who is Millie? Will Millie come here?" After pointing out that it was "Millie" and not another child who answered by that name, ask the child to help you play a game.

Write the child's name on a name tag and attach it to the front of his or her clothing. Then ask the children what else they know about this person besides the name label. Elicit answers that fully describe the child: a girl, blond hair, freckles, pink dress, etc.

Repeat the procedure with other children as long as interest is high. Point out that there are many more words they can use to describe one another than just their names. Help the children see that these attributes and qualities are what we think about when our names are spoken.

Extension Activity

Have the children use descriptive words to compare two children. Ask them to say how the two are alike and how they are different.

CHAPTER 3

Relationships with Others Activities

Everybody Soup

The children will contribute their favorite ingredients to a pot of soup and learn cooperation in preparing the final product.

Materials

- Stove or hot plate
- Kitchen utensils for soup preparation and cooking
- Large soup pot
- Soup bowls and spoons
- Extra vegetables in case some children forget to bring theirs
- Beef or chicken bouillon or other "starter"
- Seasonings

Activity

The children first discuss what it means to cooperate in order to achieve a final product everyone can enjoy. Then they each choose their favorite ingredient to contribute to a pot of "Everybody Soup." On cooking day they bring their ingredients to class and share in the preparation of the soup. After enjoying the final product, they discuss how each contributed something special and cooperated in a joint task.

Procedures

Before cooking the soup, discuss with children what it means to cooperate in achieving a final product, such as building a house, cleaning the kitchen, and so forth. Explain that they will all cooperate in making some "Everybody Soup." Point out that for "Everybody Soup" everybody gets to put in his or her favorite ingredients, which are mixed together into something everybody can enjoy. Discuss the different ingredients that can go into soup: carrots, potatoes, macaroni, celery, tomatoes. Have each child then decide on a favorite ingredient to bring to class. Send notes home with the children describing the activity and the food item.

On cooking day have the children show the others the ingredients they have brought for the soup.

Guide the food preparation. Have each child prepare his or her contribution. Use caution with peeling and cutting instruments. Put prepared food together in plastic bags until ready for cooking. Children should see their favorite things go into the one big pot.

Serve the cooked soup to each child. Discuss how each contributed something different yet all worked together in order to complete the task.

Extension Activity

Have the children engage in other cooperative tasks where each contributes something special to the group effort. For example, when cleaning up after playtime one child puts things away, another sweeps up, and so forth.

Groups Can Be Fun

The children expand their understanding of things that contribute to working together and the success of groups.

Materials

- A box containing at least twelve rocks of varying sizes, twelve buttons of varying sizes, twelve thread spools of varying sizes (or other available objects)

Activity

The children arrange three kinds of objects into three groups and describe how the objects within each group are similar and different. They discuss how the groups of children in their school are similar and different. They then identify things that prevent groups from being successful and things that contribute to group success.

Procedures

Select three students to remove the objects from the box and arrange them in three groups. Lead them to discover that each group is different from the other two, but that within each of the groups there are similarities and differences. Ask students to share their perceptions of how the objects within each group are similar (all rocks, all buttons, all spools, etc.) but in some instances different (size, shape, color, etc.).

Point out that the children in their school are arranged into groups, that each group includes boys and girls, but the boys and girls within each group are different in height, hair color, skin color, weight, and particularly in their interests. Discuss with the children ways they are different from each other and ways they can be successful in group situations. Ask questions such as the following to help them identify things that can prevent their group from being successful and things that can contribute to their group's success.

> Why do you think all children in a group need to cooperate with each other?
> Are groups fun when some children do only what they want to do?
> How does listening to the teacher help a group be successful?
> How does listening to each other help a group be successful?
> In what way will recognizing the interests of others help groups be fun?

Help the children expand their understanding of the value of group activity and ways they can contribute to the success of groups.

Extension Activity

Tell the children that they may each choose one of two activities for a twenty-minute period: art work (paints, crayons, etc.) or building (blocks, building sets, etc.). Divide the children into two groups according to their interests. Ask each of the groups (art, building) to name ways they can cooperate to help their group have an enjoyable activity (sharing, taking turns, etc.). Monitor both groups as they work, reminding them as necesary of the need to cooperate. Positively reinforce actions you observe that contribute to a healthy group climate.

Rules Are Valuable for Everyone

The children will learn to value the rules that give direction to their lives.

Activity

The children expand their understanding of the importance and value of rules to their many activities. They consider school rules to identify possible outcomes if the rules did not exist; they also discuss before and after playing a game the value of rules to the success of the game they played.

Procedures

Explain the meaning of the word *rules.* Cite several examples of school rules that are familiar to the children. Ask the children to tell why they think schools have rules. Guide their perceptions to conclude that rules (1) describe proper conduct and action, (2) suggest procedures for solving problems, (3) protect the rights and privileges of every person, (4) help to ensure safety, and (5) make it possible for groups of people to successfully do things together.

Select three school rules such as the following and discuss with the children what might happen if they did not have these rules.

> RULE: *No running up or down stairs.* Children who run might fall or push other children down stairs, causing them to be injured.)
> RULE: *Put all rubbish in rubbish cans.* (Otherwise the school would be ugly, dirty, and not a fun place to learn and play.)
> RULE: *No eating of food except in assigned areas.* (Carpets, floors, and furniture could become soiled and smelly and attract ants and other insects.)

Involve the children in playing a familiar game. Review the rules of the game before they play. After playing, discuss the value of rules to the success of the game, and how the game may not have been an enjoyable experience for all without everyone's observing the rules.

Extension Activity

Ask the children to look carefully as they go to and from school (walking, riding in a car) for several days to learn what rules control their movement and the unsafe conditions that could result if the rules were not in effect. Rules associated with seat belts, stoplights, pedestrian crossings, speed limits, stop signs, and looking before crossing even when having the right of way could be discussed. In each instance, stress the value of the rules to the children's individual safety.

Helping Others to Be Happy Makes Me Happy

The children expand their understanding of ways their actions can influence how others feel and how they feel about themselves.

Activity

The children use facial expressions to show various emotions. They then describe things that cause people to feel as they do, identifying things they do that cause other children, parents, and their teacher to become angry. They later plan ways to make other children in the school feel happy to learn how they personally feel afterwards.

Procedures

Ask the children to show angry, sad, happy, and surprised facial expressions. Invite them to describe some of the things that make them feel angry (such as other children who will not take turns or share toys). They should also describe things that result in their feeling surprised (a surprise visit by a friend), happy (a trip to the beach or park), and sad (a best friend moves away), etc.

Discuss with the children things they can do to make other children in their school happy (helping them when they need help, taking turns, sharing objects, having interest in the needs of others, etc.). Suggest that during the next two days they each plan to do something to make someone in the school happy. Follow up later and have the children describe what they did, if they believe they succeeded, and the personal feelings they had afterwards. Point out how helping others feel happy brings about a personal satisfaction and happiness.

Extension Activity

Ask the children to identify something they have been doing that causes their parents to become angry. The goal is for them to change their behavior on a trial basis to make their parents happy rather than angry. Encourage them to do this to find out how the change makes them feel about themselves.

Helpers

The children will expand their awareness of the importance of helping others.

Materials

- Paste
- Scissors
- 8½″ × 11″ sheet of paper
- Magazine pages or cutouts (pictures of men, women, children, pets, etc., for a family collage)

Activity

The children assume in-school helping roles to build understanding of how helping others contributes to the development of a positive self-concept. They also create family collages to identify various ways family members help each other and to learn how they might expand their own roles as helpers for family members.

Procedures

Involve one or more children in helping you move a piece of furniture, books, blocks, or other items to a new location. Ask the children who observed the activity to tell why they believe it was important for some of the children to help you (save time, need more than two hands, concern for the needs of others, desire to help, feel good when helping others, etc.).

Assign half the children in your group to a variety of tasks such as emptying wastepaper baskets, wiping tabletops, tidying up activity areas, storing items in boxes, watering plants, etc. The other children should serve as helpers to those assigned the tasks. Discuss with both groups of children the role of helpers before they work to complete tasks.

Provide materials for the children to create family collages. They should cut out pictures to represent each family member who lives in their home. When they complete the collages, they could take turns describing how each family member helps the family in some way (earning money, preparing meals, helping with chores around home, feeding pets, helping younger children, etc.). The goal is to help the children expand their understanding of how families should and do help each other in a variety of ways. Also, point out how helping others results in the helpers having good feelings about themselves.

Extension Activity

Prepare a card for each of the children on which is listed specific tasks they do at home to help parents, brothers and sisters, or others living with them. Discuss with the children possible ways they could expand their roles as helpers at home. Update the cards periodically by adding new helping roles they have assumed and deleting those that are no longer applicable. The purpose is to have a continued focus on the importance of contributing to the family as a helper.

Sometimes We Can Share without Talking

The children will learn that they can communicate their feelings nonverbally.

Activity

The children imagine what it would feel like to be unable to talk. They identify the meaning of common gestures, then roleplay how people can communicate feelings without words.

Procedures

Ask the children to imagine how it would feel if they could not talk. You could mention here that there are people who cannot talk because there is something physically wrong with the parts of their bodies that help us talk. Discuss how they would tell someone something without speaking. How, for example, would they show a friend that they were cold, or happy, or sad? Have the children demonstrate different ways to communicate these feelings.

After this discussion, show the children some common gestures and ask them to interpret the meaning. For example:

Nod head (yes)

Shake head (no)

Wave (goodbye)

Wave (hello)

Hug and pat (don't cry)

Hug and kiss (I love you)

Wag index finger (no, no)

If the group is still interested, direct questions or statements at individual children and have them answer without speaking. Then ask other children to guess what the answers were. For example:

Did you brush your teeth this morning?

Are you wearing a red ribbon?

Show me that you are sad.

Show me that you are happy.

How old are you?

Extension Activity

Invite someone who uses sign language to your class to demonstrate some simple signs. The children might be taught how to sign a simple message, such as "I am happy."

Feeling Happy, or Feeling Sad?

The children will learn to recognize how things said or done by one person can affect others' feelings.

Materials

- Storybook that includes a story of "Cinderella" appropriate for young children

Activity

The children listen to the reading of "Cinderella" and identify statements or actions by characters in the story that made others feel happy or sad. They then consider how the things they say or do can cause others to feel happy or sad.

Procedures

Before reading the story to the children, discuss with them how the things people say or do may make others feel happy or sad. Use illustrations of recent events in the school that may be familiar to the children (without giving names of individuals) to expand their understanding of this principle.

Ask the children to listen carefully while you read the story of Cinderella. At any point in the story they recognize something said or done to make somebody else feel happy or sad, they should raise their hands and upon being recognized describe the event in their own words. Because the story versions of "Cinderella" differ, a general summary of events that will relate to most versions is provided as a reminder list for you.

Feeling Happy	*Feeling Sad*
–Stepsisters invited to the king's grand ball.	–Stepmother saying and doing unkind things to Cinderella.
–Cinderella helping to make peace between stepsisters and prepare them for the ball.	–One stepsister telling Cinderella that if she went to the ball people would laugh (because she was a lowly cindermaid).
–Fairy godmother telling Cinderella that she will go to the ball.	–The elder stepsister, Lady Javotte, laughing and saying she would never loan her dress to Cinderella.
–Fairy godmother turning pumpkin, mice, rats, lizards into a coach with attendants.	–The stepsisters laughing when Cinderella asked if she could try on the glass slipper.
–Ways Cinderella was treated by all the people at the ball.	–Stepsisters begging Cinderella for forgiveness.
–Cinderella forgiving the stepsisters.	

Should the children fail to recognize some of the subtleties of behavior in the version of the story you read, use prompter questions to stimulate thought and help them discover those actions or statements that caused others to feel happy or sad.

Follow up the story with a discussion of how the things children may say (or do) to other children, parents, teachers, neighbors, and others can result in others feeling happy or sad. Lead them to the conclusion that people are happier when they help to make others happy rather than sad.

Extension Activity

Read another story such as "Snow White and the Seven Dwarfs," and follow the same general procedures as for "Cinderella." As the children identify things said or done that made others feel sad, for instance, ask them to tell how the statement or action could be changed to make the other person feel happy instead of sad. Use the same procedure to identify ways our actions can cause happy feelings to become sad feelings.

Planting, Growing, Tending, and Sharing

The children will learn how cooperative activity by a group can produce positive results.

Materials

- Designated outdoor area for a miniature garden, or containers filled with soil
- Seeds, seedlings, cuttings, etc.
- Tools
- Water (containers or watering hose)
- Fertilizer

Activity

The children assume responsibilities for various kinds of work required to plant a miniature garden and provide continual care for it. They discuss ways they demonstrated a cooperative spirit in the project. They also discuss where a cooperative spirit was lacking and ways they could improve group undertakings in the future.

Procedures

(Students should have completed "Let's Grow a Garden," p. 164, before beginning this activity.)

Establish a mood for cooperative activity to begin work on a miniature garden. Help the children decide who will do what to plant the seeds (seedlings, cuttings, etc.). These jobs should be identified as follows.

Gathering tools and all other needed items.

Weeding (if necessary).

Loosening of soil or filling containers with soil.

Making small holes at right depth for kind of seed, seedling, cutting being planted.

Placing seeds, seedlings, cuttings in holes, filling holes, and firming soil around them.

Providing containers of water.

Returning tools and other items to storage areas.

Cleaning up after the garden is planted.

Emphasize throughout the planting and cleanup experience the need for group cooperation and the value in all children's helping to pursue and accomplish a goal.

After the cleanup is completed and all items stored, discuss with the children ways they shared equally and cooperated in the group project. Also discuss procedures (if any) where sharing and a cooperative spirit were lacking. Have them identify ways problem areas could be reduced or eliminated in the future.

Follow up this activity by having children continue to monitor the growth of their garden, assigning work such as watering, adding soil, weeding, and/or fertilizing as needed.

Extension Activity

When the plants have grown to maturity, invite other classes and/or parents to hear children explain how they proceeded to create a garden and the ways they had to cooperate to be successful. They should also describe how they had to assume responsibilities for the continuing care of the garden.

We Appreciate the Efforts of Others

The children will learn to value and show their appreciation for efforts made to communicate with others.

Activity

The children identify a selected object, which you describe using body motions. They then play a game in which they each use motions to describe an object. The other children watch and identify the object described. Throughout the activity emphasis is made on developing an awareness of and an appreciation for the efforts made by others to communicate.

Procedures

Select five objects from your classroom (book, ball, pencil, Tinker Toy, building block, etc.) and place them on the floor or on a table in front of the children. Use whatever movements you feel are appropriate to describe one of the objects. When you finish your description, the children are to identify the object you described. Invite two children to take turns performing movements to describe two of the remaining four objects. Emphasize the need to carefully watch the child doing the movements and to understand the description being communicated.

Ask each child to select an object not included among the five objects selected earlier. Encourage them to think of motions they might use to describe the objects they selected. Then plan a presentation in which each child will place the selected object among all the others and take turns performing their motions. Before the presentation begins, discuss with the children how they can show their appreciation for each person as the objects are described. Remaining quiet and still, watching respectfully, withholding all comments until afterwards, applauding at appropriate times, and not interfering in any way with efforts made by others are some of the ways they can show their appreciation.

Have the children make their presentations. The objects are to be identified by the other children only after each presentation is completed. Afterwards discuss with them ways they showed their appreciation for the efforts of others and ways a lack of appreciation (if any) was shown.

Extension Activity

Invite someone experienced in pantomime to perform for your children. Request that activities be pantomimed that the children are likely to recognize. Afterwards discuss ways the children showed their appreciation for the performances and how they might improve their expressions of appreciation in the future.

Family Pretend

The children will learn to recognize through dramatic play various family roles.

Materials

- Simple hand puppets, one for each member of the family (father, mother, older sister, grandparents, etc.), constructed from socks, yarn, buttons, and fabric

Activity

The children meet a family of puppets. They make up things each family member might say. The children each select a family member whose part they want to play. They are given problem situations that they then act out together.

Procedures

Introduce the puppet family to the children. As you introduce each member, ask the children to tell you something that family member would say. Hold up the puppet and repeat the line to the group.

Let each child select a family member whose part he or she would like to play. Present one of the following situations or one of your own. Discuss each briefly, then have the children act one out. If you are working with a larger group, have the rest of the class act as an audience. Repeat the procedure as long as interest holds.

    One of the children fell and hurt his or her knee.

    It's Daddy's turn to cook but he's late getting home. What shall we do?

    Grandpa lost his glasses and he's very upset.

    Mommy comes home and finds her lamp broken.

Extension Activity

Read to the children Charlotte Zolotow's *A Father Like That* (New York: Harper & Row, 1971) about a little boy who wants a father so much he fantasizes about how perfect his father would be. After reading the story, discuss what the little boy wants and what his mother does to make him feel better.

Other good books on families to read and discuss are: *The Sorely Trying Day*, Russell and Lillian Hoban (New York: Harper & Row, 1964), which shows how family members react in the face of conflict, and *Families Live Together*, Esther K. Meeks and Elizabeth Bagwell (New York: Follett, 1969).

Cumulative Drawings...
and Courtesies

The children will learn to identify ways they were courteous and/or discourteous during a cumulative drawing activity.

Materials

- Index cards with scribbles (one for each child)
- Felt-tip pens
- Chalkboard and chalk (or large sheet of paper and crayons)

Activity

The children contribute to a cumulative drawing on the chalkboard. Then in small groups they participate in a cumulative drawing activity using index cards, passing the cards to each other on your cue. They later reflect on the experience and use it as a basis for discussing ways they could demonstrate more courtesy in group situations for future cumulative drawings and other kinds of activities.

Procedures

Draw a large rectangle on the chalkboard (or on a large sheet of paper) and a simple scribble inside the rectangle. Then invite several children, one at a time, to add to your scribble to create a design or picture of some kind.

Organize the children in groups of five. Each child in each group should be given a felt-tip pen and an index card with a scribble on it. The children sit in a circle; on your cue they add lines to the scribble. After a brief period, and again on your cue, they pass their cards to the right. They then add lines to the new cards they have. This procedure continues until all five children have contributed to each of the cards. The cards are then displayed so they can be enjoyed by all the children. Throughout the procedures observe how the children relate to each other to complete the drawings.

Ask the children to identify some courtesies they might show during future cumulative drawing activities (and activities in general). Guide them to identify such things as passing the cards on your cues, gently passing the cards and not throwing them, passing the cards in a position so the next child can easily begin work, using lines that will contribute to the drawing and not destroying what another child has contributed, returning the felt-tip pens to the designated location, not making fun of the lines another child has drawn, etc. Point out how in group activities courtesies on the part of each child will contribute to the enjoyment of all and help everyone have a good feeling about the experience.

Extension Activity

Make available a large sheet of paper and crayons. Invite the children to contribute to a cumulative drawing mural. Have one child use a crayon and begin the drawing with a scribble. Before the other children begin contributing to the drawing, ask them to suggest ways they can extend courtesies to each other throughout the activity. As they add to the drawing, help them focus on situations in which courtesy needs to be shown so that all the children will feel they are equal contributors. Display the drawing and describe the cooperative group effort that made it possible.

Manners Game

The children will learn how good manners are important in our relationships with others.

Activity

Through discussion the children are introduced to the concept of manners and the importance of good manners to our relationships with other people. After hearing situations by the teacher, they tell about what they would do and/or say to resolve situations by demonstrating good manners.

Procedures

Explain to the children that the ways we act when we are with other people can result in others accepting or rejecting us in the future. Also point out how we feel better about ourselves when others are pleased with rather than disappointed in our behavior. Introduce the idea of manners as those behaviors that help us to get along with people we know and those we do not know.

Read each of the following situations twice. After each situation is read, select one child to suggest something to say or do that will show good manners.

Suzy bumped into Robert. What should Suzy say? ("Excuse me please," "I'm sorry," etc.)

Terry wants Koreen to pass the juice. What should Terry say to Koreen? What should he say after she passes the juice? ("Please pass the juice," "Thank you," etc.)

Carol makes a loud, disturbing noise by sliding her chair while the teacher is talking. What should she say? ("Excuse me please," "Oops, I'm sorry," etc.)

Alan takes Donna's book by mistake and Donna is unhappy. What should Alan say to Donna? ("I'm sorry I took your book," "Excuse me, I didn't mean to," etc.)

David drops his favorite pen but doesn't know it. Collette saw him drop it. What should Collette do? (Pick up the pen, give it to David, tell him he dropped it.)

Ralph sees a very old woman opening a door to pass through. What should Ralph do? (Hold the door open until the woman passes through.)

A neighbor is upset because Lorraine is playing her radio very loud. What should Lorraine do and say after the neighbor complains? (Turn down the radio; apologize to the neighbor for the disturbance.)

It is recommended that you improvise other situations that will help the children focus on ways to show good manners. Eventually, the children will see that "good" manners always take the other person's feelings into account.

Extension Activity

Ask the children to watch people (family members, people in stores, etc.) closely during the next few days for both good and bad manners they demonstrate. Then have them share their observations. They should describe the good manners they observed, then the bad manners. For the bad manners, ask them to tell what they would have done to show good manners.

Friendships Near and Far

The children will learn how their thoughts can be sent through the mail to reach others and establish new friendships.

Materials

- Paper and envelopes (or postcards)
- Stamps
- Letter written to the children from the teacher

Activity

The children discuss how the mail carrier helps people stay in touch with one another through letters. They listen to a letter read to them by the teacher, then compose a group letter to the children in another preschool. When the return letter arrives, they listen to it together.

Procedures

Ask the children about their mail carrier, when he or she brings the mail, the kinds of things he or she brings, etc. Guide them to see that the mail carrier delivers letters from near and far that help people keep in touch with one another. Read the children a letter you have written to them. It might begin:

> Dear Children,
>
> I was just thinking how happy I am to be your teacher. John comes every morning with a happy face. Sandy helps me straighten the block corner. Marybeth likes to climb high on the jungle gym. Timmy is not afraid to try new foods. Joy likes stories...etc.
>
> Your teacher,
>
> Mr. Johnson

Arrange ahead of time an exchange of letters with children in another preschool. With the children, compose a letter to these new friends. Encourage everyone to contribute something special to this group letter, guiding the children to ask questions of their new friends and also tell something of themselves. If the children can write their names, have them each sign the letter. Explain that their new friends will answer soon.

When the return letter arrives, read it aloud. Compose an answer together and keep the correspondence going.

Extension Activity

Take the children on an excursion to a nearby post office to see the skills and tasks involved in postal work. Try to plan the trip for the day you mail the return letter.

We're Quiet When It's Someone's Turn to Talk

The children will learn that listening courteously can be important.

Materials

- Guitar or drum

Activity

The children play a game in which they have to listen carefully in order to stop moving when the music stops. They discuss why some children kept moving and others didn't, and they learn that listening can be important. They then discuss situations in which they listen while someone else talks.

Procedures

Sing a lively song such as "When the Saints Go Marching In" several times while accompanying yourself on the guitar, drum, or another instrument. Invite the children to play a listening game. They move to the music as long as you are singing and playing but stop moving and remain still when there is silence. When you stop, remain silent for several moments to see who the good listeners are.

Guide a brief discussion on listening with these questions.

Why did some children keep moving when others stopped as they should? (They weren't listening closely enough.)

When is it important to listen? (When someone's talking, when learning words to a song, story time, in church, etc.)

Extension Activity

Make the game more challenging by singing the song while tapping a drum. The children are to stop moving when you stop tapping the drum but continue to sing.

Sometimes Fast, Sometimes Slow Game

The children will learn that there are appropriate times and places for moving fast and slow.

Materials

- Drum and mallet

Activity

The children begin by identifying places where running is appropriate and safe and places where it is not. They play a game in which they move in tempo to the beat of a drum, covering a range of movement from fast to slow. They then take turns experimenting with different tempos and conclude the activity by matching tempos to different situations.

Procedure

Begin by asking the children to identify places where it's safe and appropriate to run (playground, beach, parks) and places where it's more appropriate to walk (inside the house, classroom, stores). Discuss reasons for taking care with their movements in some places (safety, bothering others, consideration of rules, etc.). Guide them to see that although it's wonderful to run and jump, sometimes they have to take care and slow down.

Invite them to play a fast/slow game. Locate the activity in an area large enough for the children to move freely. Tell the children your drum will tell them how to move. To illustrate, play the drum with a fast beat, then a slow beat; then invite the children to move in tempo. Continue the game using a variety of patterns including random fast and slow, beats that speed up, and beats that slow down.

Invite the children to take turns beating the drum. Let them invent their own rhythms at first. Then add cues such as "Let's hear a beat for running in the playground," or "Let's hear a beat for walking into church." The children should agree on the appropriateness of movement for each situation.

Conclude the activity by having the children tell you why it is safe to move fast in some places but not in others.

Extension Activity

Add a loud-soft dimension to the game, in which the children move noisily or quietly to the beat as well as fast or slow. Give the children situations calling for appropriate loud-soft, fast-slow behaviors. Later have them explain why they need to move quietly in some places.

I Can Use the Telephone!

The children will learn simple telephone courtesies.

Materials

- Two toy telephones

Activity

The children first take the role of receivers, with the teacher as caller, and engage in a telephone dialogue. They then talk about appropriate telephone responses to give when an adult who receives a call is not at home.

Procedures

Have one child take the role of a child who answers the phone, another child the role of an adult who is the caller. The caller engages the child in a telephone dialogue in which a request is made to speak to an adult in the household.

> Ring!
> Child: Hello.
> Caller: Hello. Is your mommy at home?
> Child: Just a minute please (calls "Mommy").
> Mommy: Hello.
> etc.

Have the two children switch roles. Repeat the game, changing your telephone behavior and the situation. For example:

> Ring!
> Child: Hello.
> Caller: Is this the Jones house?
> Child: Yes.
> Caller: Can I speak to your daddy?
> Child: He can't come to the phone now.
> etc.

Discuss helpful telephone courtesies: saying "hello" when you pick up the receiver, saying "just a minute" when calling mommy or daddy to the phone, etc.

Extension Activity

Encourage interested children to learn their phone numbers and help them practice dialing the numbers on a toy telephone.

Balloon Tap Game

The children will increase their understanding of the value of following rules to group participation in a game.

Materials

- Three inflated, round balloons approximately twelve inches in diameter
- Masking tape

Activity

The children are organized into two teams and the rules for a game explained. They then play the game, later discussing how the rules made it possible for all to participate equally. Relationships are drawn between following rules and making games enjoyable for all who play.

Procedures

Introduce the balloon tap game by organizing the children in playing positions and reviewing the rules of the game. Two equal teams of children should be organized as follows:

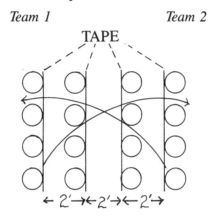

The two teams stand facing each other with toes touching the tape. Players must keep both feet on the floor in a stationary position at all times. Two or three balloons are tossed up between the two teams. The object is to hit the balloons over the heads of the back-row players for each game. If a balloon falls to the floor it can be picked up and hit again as long as the player's feet stay in position. The team that hits the most balloons over the heads of the back-row players wins the game. As points are scored, the balloons are retrieved and again tossed up between the teams until the game ends.

Conclude the activity by focusing the children's attention on the value of rules to ensuring that games are fun for all players. Also focus their attention on problems that arise when one or more players choose not to follow the rules. As much as possible, show direct relationships between following rules and making games fun for all.

Extension Activity

Ask the children if they believe it would be more fun to play the game without one or more of the rules and/or if one or more of the rules were changed. Try their suggestions (or your own) during another playing of the game. Then discuss with them how the changes helped (or hindered) the players have fun during the game.

Find and Match the Squares Game

The children will learn the value of fairness in playing games.

Materials

- Two large sheets of paper 3' × 3' (ten different sizes of squares are cut from each sheet; the squares are preserved for use in a game)

Activity

The children are divided into two equal groups. They learn to play a game that requires finding paper squares placed at different locations in the room and then matching the squares in spaces on a large sheet of paper. Following the game they discuss how the game could be played to ensure "fairness" for all participants. They then play the game again, incorporating aspects of fairness discussed.

Procedures

Divide the children into two equal groups, each with a group leader. The group leaders sit with their groups on opposite sides of the room. As the children close their eyes, place the twenty different squares cut from the two sheets in easy-to-find locations of the room. Then give each group leader one of the large sheets, which is to be placed on the floor or on a table. On your signal, group members are to begin searching the room for squares. As the children find squares, they take them to the group leaders (a child may take only one square at a time to the group leader). The leader tries to fit the square into one of the spaces of the large sheet. If the square fits, it is kept in position. If it does not fit, it is returned to the location where the child found it. The game continues until one group has found and correctly placed all the squares in the proper positions.

After the game has ended, discuss with the children the idea of fairness. Have them suggest things game players could do to make the game fair for everybody (help keep the squares from becoming damaged so they will fit properly, return squares that do not fit as soon as possible so the other group will have an equal chance, show courtesy in moving about the room to prevent others from being "bumped" or detained in some way, be patient as the group leader tries to fit the square into a space on the sheet, etc.). Expand their understanding of fairness in terms of impartiality, honesty, conformity to rules, etc.

Following the discussion, organize new groups and have them play the game again, making every attempt to have as fair a situation as possible.

Extension Activity

Ask the children to describe things they could do at the playground to create a fair situation for all. List their ideas, then take them to the playground and ask them to demonstrate each of the things they named. The goal is for you to act in need of understanding, and they will help you to understand.

Getting to Know You ... and Others

The children will learn new information about each other and develop a greater acceptance for the interests of others.

Activity

Working in pairs, the children tell each other five things about themselves. They then share the things they learned about their partners with all of the children in the group. The purpose is to develop a deeper concern for and acceptance of the unique interests and characteristics of all children in the group.

Procedures

Organize the children in pairs. As much as possible, pair the children who do not seem to know each other well. The pairs of children are to learn five new things about each other, which they will share with the other children. Questions such as the following could be used to prompt their interviews of each other.

> What is your favorite food?
>
> Do you have brothers and sisters? How many?
>
> What is your favorite game?
>
> What is your favorite activity in school? at home?
>
> What is your favorite color?
>
> Where do you live?

A goal is for the children to share things about themselves but have another person do the "telling." This approach is recommended to build a spirit of community among the children and promote a higher level of acceptance of each other through "knowing." Repeat the activity periodically with different pairs of students and questions designed to reveal new information about each other. Help the children develop a greater interest in and acceptance for individual preferences.

Extension Activity

Make a plan for the children to interview their parents and learn five things they can tell about in class. Hobbies, types of work, birthplaces, favorite sports, favorite TV programs, favorite kinds of cars, and other such categories of interest could be reported the next day.

Gifts Make Us All Feel Good

The children will learn to recognize the "feeling" value in giving and receiving gifts.

Materials

- Materials required to prepare gifts

Activity

The children discuss reasons for giving gifts and the kinds of feelings people who receive and give gifts have. They then make gifts, which they give to selected members of their families, and later discuss the reactions of those who received the gifts and their own feelings as givers.

Procedures

Involve the children in a discussion about receiving gifts and how receiving gifts makes people feel. Explain that gifts are ways people express love, thoughtfulness, appreciation, gratitude, kindness, etc. You might have each child in the group tell about the best gift he or she received and how the gift made him or her feel.

Plan an activity with the children in which they will each prepare an example of their schoolwork (art, lettering, crafts, etc.) to give as a gift to selected members of their families. Stress the need to make the gifts as nice as possible; encourage meticulous care to achieve the very best results.

When the gifts are completed, prepare a brief note similar to the following to be attached to each gift: "Please accept this gift from (name) to you." After the children have presented their gifts, have them share their experiences. "Did the person feel happy when you gave the gift?" "Did the person say 'thank you'?" "Did the person ask questions about the gift?" "What questions?" "How did you feel after giving the gift?"

For a concluding discussion, ask the children to share how they felt when they gave their gifts and observed the happiness another person had. Lead them to an understanding of how making the receiver happy makes the giver happy, too.

Extension Activity

Have the children identify a person connected with the school in some way (director, custodian, parent helper, resource person, etc.) as one to whom they wish to give a gift. When the gift has been prepared (class project suggested), arrange for the person to visit the class to receive the gift. Afterwards, discuss with the children the gift receiver's reaction and how they felt about giving the gift.

Showing Respect: The Only Way to Go

The children will learn to recognize the value of showing respect in relations with others.

Activity

The children are asked to reveal how they could show respect in a series of given situations. The importance of being exemplars of respectful behavior is presented as a way of providing positive models for others to emulate.

Procedures

Use the following situations (or others you believe are more appropriate) to stimulate discussion about showing respect in relations with others. Ask the children the following questions.

What would you do if:

You wanted to tell your mother something but she was talking on the telephone?

You were trying to tell somebody something but another child kept interrupting?

Somebody got a cut while playing on the swing?

All the children were taking naps but you did not feel sleepy and wanted to go out and play?

There were only two cookies left and three children wanted to eat them?

You were waiting a turn to ride the seesaw but others jumped in line in front of you?

A child in your group lost something and was crying?

A child pushed you, believing you had already pushed another child?

A teacher scolded you for something you did not do?

Another child said something about you that was not true?

Accept all responses to the ten situations, but use the children's responses as springboards for discussing ways to show respect while responding to any situation. Point out the contagious aspect of respect, that others are more likely to show kindness and respect when we do. Stress the need to "model" respectful behavior in all situations to help others learn how to show respect.

Extension Activity

Stage several hypothetical situations similar to the ten presented earlier. Have the children role-play how to show respect rather than simply discuss what they might do. Suggest alternative behaviors when appropriate.

Asking for Help

The children will learn the value of asking for help when they cannot do something themselves.

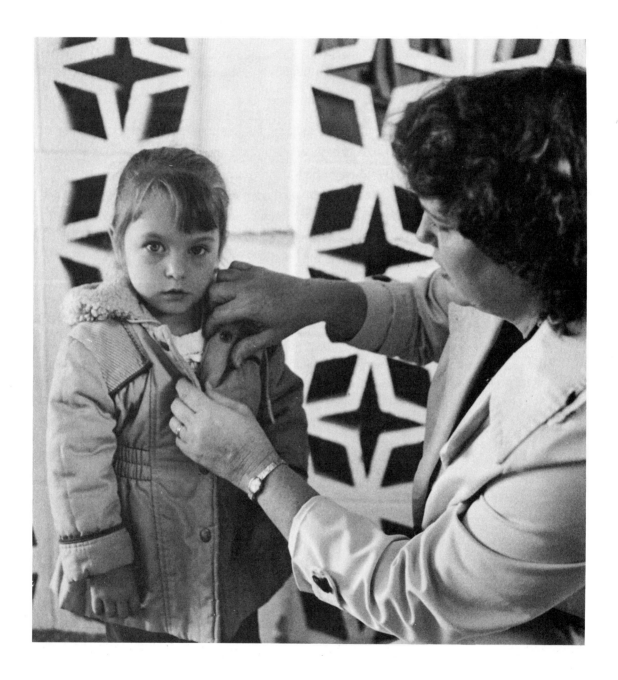

Materials

- Pair of child's sneakers with laces
- Sweater with buttons down the front
- Pullover with long sleeves and a small neckline
- Dress with sash that ties in the back
- Pants with zipper and button at the waist

Activity

The children discuss dressing tasks that are difficult for them to complete by themselves and identify the people who help them with these difficulties. Volunteers select one or more items, attempt to put them on, then ask for help when they get stuck. They discuss different help-seeking approaches and learn that asking for help is something everyone has to do at some time. They then identify school tasks that sometimes require help.

Procedures

In a group discussion, point out to the children that some things are hard to do all by oneself. Briefly discuss who helps them get dressed in the morning and what this person does to make the task easier. Invite volunteers to select one or more items and try to put them on. They should ask you for help at the point where they begin to experience difficulty.

Call attention to how each child approaches the problem of seeking help. You might say for example, how John can pull his pants on but needs help with the button, or how Mary needs help buttoning the little buttons close to her neck. Gently encourage the children to verbalize the help they require.

Point out that everyone — even adults — needs to ask for help sometimes. Elicit examples from the children of times when their parents, siblings, or friends need help. Remind children that part of your job is to help them when they run into difficulty with school tasks.

Discuss some of the school activities that require someone else's help, such as reading a book, completing a difficult puzzle, swinging on a swing, and playing dolls. Point out that part of learning is knowing when help is needed.

Extension Activity

Be alert for occasions when the children can be of help to one another. Frame your requests in a manner that asks them to support those in need. Use gentle encouragement: "Margaret could use a hand putting those blocks away," "Can you help Mary push the wagon in the closet?", etc.

CHAPTER 4

Relationships with Others Activities

(Respect for Differences in Others)

We All Need to Help Each Other

The children will develop positive attitudes toward and an awareness of problems physically handicapped persons face.

Materials

- Blindfolds

Activity

The children identify and discuss physically handicapping conditions they know about. They take turns wearing blindfolds to simulate activities of the blind. From the experience they associate specific problems with being blind and use the information to discuss problems of other handicapping conditions.

Procedures

Ask the children if they know or have seen someone who has a physical handicap. Have them describe handicaps they have observed (missing limb, blindness, deafness, paralyzed legs, etc.) and identify what they believe are some of the special problems disabled persons encounter.

Place a blindfold on a child who volunteers to assist you. As the other children watch, lead the child with the blindfold on a short walk. After the blindfold is removed ask the child to describe how it feels not being able to see. Invite other volunteers to take turns wearing a blindfold, walk across the room, pick up a selected item, then return to the starting place. You and the children watching should serve as protectors to prevent injury by those who wear blindfolds. Coach from the sidelines if appropriate.

Discuss with the child what they believe are special problems blind people have when eating, working, bathing, going places other than where they live, and taking care of things they own. Use this same approach to discuss special problems associated with other handicapping situations. If possible, invite a handicapped person to visit your class to tell about the problems of being handicapped and to answer questions children might want to ask.

Throughout the procedures make every attempt to build a positive attitude of concern for the problems of the physically handicapped and recognition of the need for those without handicaps to provide assistance when possible.

Extension Activity

Take the children on a trip to a rehabilitation center where they may see and talk with people who have handicapping conditions. Ask a representative of the center to explain to the children why such centers are needed and how centers help handicapped persons.

We All Deserve Equal Opportunities

The children will build positive attitudes toward equal work opportunities for men and women and the elimination of sex-role stereotyping.

Materials

- Collection of magazines (or a collection of pictures cut out from magazines) showing men and women in a variety of work roles
- Scissors (if pictures need to be cut out of magazines)

Activity

The children will identify things they do to help at home and consider which were named by boys, which were named by girls, and how both boys and girls are equally capable of helping in the same way. They sort a collection of pictures into women's and men's work roles and then discuss the kinds of tasks illustrated in each picture to counter problems of sex-role stereotyping in work.

Procedures

Ask the children to name some things they do at home to help their parents, brothers and sisters, grandparents, and others. Make a list of the things mentioned and categorize them as named by boy or girl. When the list is complete, identfy those named by both boys and girls. Then identify the things that only girls named and ask if boys are capable of doing the same things. Follow the same procedure for naming things mentioned only by boys. Point out during the discussion that boys and girls are equally capable of helping in the same ways.

Invite the children to help you arrange the collection of pictures into two displays (floor, wall, etc.). One display should show women working and the other, men working. Ask the children to look at the two displays to learn if any of the pictures show men and women in the same work role. Then hold up each of the pictures in the display showing women working and ask the children if they think men could do the same job. If a response of "no" is given, ask them to tell why they gave that response. Follow the same procedure to ask them whether they believe women could do the same jobs men are shown doing. Throughout the procedures make every attempt to build positive attitudes among the children toward the elimination of sex-role stereotyping in work roles. Emphasize that many jobs usually done by men also could be done by women; many jobs usually done by women also could be done by men.

Extension Activity

Invite to your class one or more women who hold jobs traditionally held by men (police officer, construction worker, etc.) to tell the children about their work and why they like it. Also invite one or more men who have jobs traditionally held by women (nurse, secretary, etc.) to tell about their work and why they like it.

Say It Another Way

The children will develop an appreciation for and some knowledge of sign language as an effective communication tool.

Activity

The children invent hand and body motions to communicate ideas. They then learn to "sign" several words using the language of the deaf and discuss how people with hearing impairments learn to communicate successfully.

Procedures

(Students should have completed "We All Need to Help Each Other," p. 88, before beginning this activity.)

Ask the children if they can show you ways to use their hands and body motions to say things without talking. You might have volunteers try to communicate these statements (or others you believe are appropriate) without talking.

I am hungry, I want to eat!

Be quiet, I am trying to sleep.

Come on, let's go out and play.

Where is my toy? Is it in this room?

Please read this book to me.

I hurt my knee.

Help me tie my shoelaces.

Will you open this for me?

Point out that many people who are deaf or who have profound hearing deficiencies could not communicate with others without using written language or hand, eye, and/or body motions. Due to the need for a language without spoken words, a sign language has been developed to aid communication between those who are deaf and between the deaf and those who can hear.

Teach the children the signs *I*, *love*, and *friends* (see blackline master no. 1 in the appendix). Conduct a drill experience by calling the words randomly and having them make the signs. Gradually increase the tempo of the drill.

Emphasize during the procedures the disadvantages in life for those with handicapping conditions but how cooperation and inventiveness can result in all people living satisfying, productive lives.

Extension Activity

Involve the children in helping you create a very brief story that includes common words and simplified actions. Invite a knowledgeable person to your class who can teach the children to sign the story. Later have students sign the words and activities as you read the story. The signed story could be performed at a parents' meeting or for other classes of children.

Culture Fair Fun

The children will develop positive attitudes toward cultural differences.

Materials

- Items needed to present a culture fair

Activity

With the help of parents and friends, a culture fair is planned and presented for the children. As the children participate in the various activities they are guided to develop an appreciation for cultural groups other than their own. They later discuss the benefits they derived from participation in the fair.

Procedures

Plan with the children, parents, and friends a culture fair during which things of interest from different cultural groups will be shared. These shared activities could include foods, dress or costumes, artifacts, performances of dance and/or music, pictures, musical instruments, jewelry, etc. This could be a large-scale fair for the entire school or a small-scale fair for one group of children. Each activity should be explained to help the children expand their understanding of differences between cultural groups and the unique contributions each group has to offer. The goal is to encourage acceptance of and appreciation for cultural differences among peoples of the world.

On a day after the fair, discuss with the children the benefits they derived from the activities. Ask them to share things they learned, and remind them of things they overlooked.

Extension Activity

From an assorted collection of activity pictures cut from magazines, ask the children to select some that represent cultures other than their own. Review their selections with them, and point out — as much as possible — cultural differences revealed in the pictures.

What Do Others Think about Me?

The children will learn that people form opinions about others by observing their behavior.

Materials

- Book with story of "Snow White and the Seven Dwarfs" (version that includes names of and information about the seven dwarfs)

Activity

After the children listen to a reading of the fairy tale, they share their opinions about why certain characters were given descriptive names. They learn that people build impressions of others by the behaviors they observe. The activity is concluded as the children pantomime descriptive behaviors of nicknames.

Procedures

Read to the children "Snow White and the Seven Dwarfs." Then help them learn to name the main characters. At an appropriate time you might want to explain that dwarfs are sometimes called "little people" because their bodies do not grow as much as some larger people. Stress the need to accept and relate to all people equally, regardless of their size or shape.

Help the children memorize the names of the seven dwarfs (Happy, Doc, Sleepy, Sneezy, Dopey, Grumpy, Bashful). When they can name all seven, ask why they think the dwarfs were given those names. Guide them to recognize that the names were related to the behavioral characteristics of the dwarfs in the story. Point out that people often observe habits and/or actions of others, form opinions, and give them names, as they did for the dwarfs (grouchy, tattle-tale, crybaby, etc.). Explain that sometimes the names make us feel good, and sometimes they make us feel bad.

As a final activity have the children as a group pantomime nicknames as you call them out (happy, grouchy, wiggly, jumpy, bossy, sneezy, sleepy, etc.). Encourage them to move and make facial expressions they believe will represent the behavior of each "character."

Extension Activity

Read other short fairy tales you believe are appropriate to help the children recognize characters by the behavior they demonstrate ("Goldilocks and the Three Bears," "The Three Billy Goats Gruff," "Little Red Riding Hood," "Pinocchio," etc.). Where appropriate, have the children as a group or individually pantomime behaviors of characters in the stories.

Things that Help when We Need Help

The children will learn to recognize that certain objects are made for the purpose of helping disabled persons overcome their handicaps.

Materials

- Pictures or drawings of objects used by disabled persons (see master no. 2 in the appendix)
- Stool or chair

Activity

The children look at pictures of various objects used by people with disabilities. They discuss how each object helps the person in question. If possible, children are provided the opportunity to examine the real items.

Procedures

Ask the children what they do when they want something that is out of their reach (ask someone for help; get a stool or chair). Demonstrate how a chair can be a tool for helping to overcome the handicap of being too short to reach some things.

Show the pictures to the children, and ask them to identify the items pictured. Discuss the disabilities associated with each thing. Guide them to discover how each item helps the user to see, hear, and move around. Lead them to see how a wheelchair can help a person without legs in the same way that a stroller can help a child who can't walk fast enough to keep up with adults.

If you can arrange to borrow one or more of the items, show them to the children. If you feel it appropriate, you might ask the children to touch, examine, and use the items. They should understand that these are not objects to be frightened of but tools to help people who need them.

Extension Activity

Invite a person in a wheelchair to visit the class and talk about problems of mobility, such as the lack of ramps in some buildings, elevator buttons located too high, water fountains, etc.

Breads Are Like People...Alike but Different

The children will develop a better awareness of the differences among various cultural groups.

Materials

- Bite-size samples of as many breads as are available from different cultures and the children's own cultures (French, Italian, Portuguese bread, unleavened bread, tortillas, sourdough, etc.)
- Assorted pictures of people from various cultural groups

Activity

The children discuss differences among people from various cultural groups and how learning things about others helps to build friendships. They then sample a variety of breads to build acceptance and greater appreciation for a food eaten by different peoples. An intended outcome is a better awareness that people are alike in some ways but different in others.

Procedures

Discuss with the children differences among people from various cultural groups (foods, clothes, dances, music, hobbies, recreation, habitats, etc.). You might then show pictures of people from different cultures. Point out how learning about others makes our world a friendlier place. You could use the example of how the children have developed close friendships with others in their group after learning things about those they consider to be their friends.

At snacktime explain to the children that you have some food from different cultural groups that you would like to share with them. Point out that bread is a food people in most cultures eat in one form or another, yet each group has a different way of preparing this basic food. Encourage each child to sample the different breads. The goal is to introduce the children to the different breads to build greater acceptance of cultures other than their own. You could later have the children discuss how the breads are different in terms of taste, appearance, texture, ingredients (if known), etc. Guide them to see that breads are like people. . .alike but also different.

Extension Activity

Plan a "share-and-tell day" when the children will bring something from either their own culture or a culture different from theirs, which they show and tell about. Send a note to parents in advance of the scheduled day to alert them to the need to prepare. Point out during the sharing session the enjoyment of learning about other people.

Family Shapes and Sizes

The children will learn that families come in all sizes and shapes; they will also begin to explore a broad definition of families.

Materials

- People shapes cut out of flannel (see master no. 3 in the appendix)
- Large flannelboard
- Two pictures of different families (see master no. 3)

Activity

Through the use of pictures illustrating two nontraditional families, the children explore the idea that families come in different shapes and sizes. Family shapes are reproduced on a flannelboard, with the children helping. They are then invited to share their own family shapes and sizes. They identify individual family members and consider the differences among families.

Procedures

Prepare enough people shapes for children to create a variety of family types. If you prefer to provide your own family pictures, be sure to consider the realities the children in your group encounter in their worlds. Avoid defining *family* in the traditional sense of father, mother, and children.

Show the children the first picture. Invite speculation about what it illustrates. After they recognize it as a family, have them identify the members pictured. If the children question the absence of a father, remind them that some families do not have fathers but are still families because they live together and help each other.

Reproduce the family shapes on the flannelboard, using one adult shape and two child shapes. You might ask the group to help you with this. Show them that the large shapes represent adults and the small ones represent children.

Show the children the second picture. Repeat the basic procedure you used with the first picture, but this time guide the children to see that this family is larger and includes parents, grandparents, and children. Reproduce this family shape on the flannelboard, using four adult and two child shapes. You might want to call on one or two volunteers to do this.

Invite two children to show their family shapes and sizes on the flannelboard. Ask them to identify family members. Discuss the similarities and differences between the two representations. Lead the children toward the idea that families can be quite different, but they are all special. Everyone belongs to a family.

Extension Activity

Encourage the children to bring in photographs of their families to share with others. Display pictures on a bulletin board under the theme "Family Shapes and Sizes."

Avoiding Sex-Role Stereotyping

The children will become aware that many career choices are open to them and that one's sex does not determine the choice of a career.

Activity

During the year the children visit several job sites. After each field trip, a man or woman not usually associated with a particular profession visits the class to talk about what he or she does.

Procedures

The best way to reverse sex-role stereotyping in career choices is to provide opportunities for the children to meet men and women who have chosen unconventional professions.

Choose several places to visit during the year: local hospital, fire station, hair salon, police station, bus company, business office. Discuss with the children what they observed: "What were the workers doing?" "What did they wear?" "What equipment and tools did they use?"

After each field trip, invite a worker to visit the classroom to talk about his or her work. For the work sites mentioned above, invite a male nurse, female firefighter, male hairdresser, female police officer, female bus driver, male secretary, or female executive. Ask the guest to bring or wear the clothing and materials associated with the job. For instance, the nurse could bring surgical hats and masks, stethoscope, and empty syringes. The worker can describe the kind of work done and talk about why he or she chose the profession.

Extension Activity

Provide a job setting in the dramatic play area. Assemble as many materials as possible to help the children recreate through play what they learned from the field trip and visitor talk. Encourage both boys and girls to take on job roles.

CHAPTER 5

Physical and Emotional Growth Activities

I Have My Own Feelings

The children become aware of their feelings and learn to be accepting of them.

Materials

- Variety of pictures from magazines, mounted on sturdy construction paper and showing degrees of five emotions: happy, sad, angry, disgusted, afraid
- Five plain, white, dinner-sized paper plates
- Wide felt-tip pen
- Hole punch
- Five thirty-inch lengths of heavy yarn

Activity

The children look at pictures and identify the emotions expressed by the people in them. They play a game in which they each choose a "feeling face," then express the emotion shown while others try to identify it.

Procedures

Draw the following "feeling faces" on the five paper plates.

Sad   *Happy*   *Angry*   *Afraid*   *Disgusted*

Make a hole at the top of each plate and tie a length of yarn in a loop that can safely and comfortably be slipped over a child's head. Set these aside.

Show the children the pictures from magazines and ask them to match each of the pictures with one of the five "feeling faces." You might ask them which pictures show people who are sad, happy, or angry or ask them to group the happy faces together, then the sad ones, and so forth. Hold up three or four pictures one by one and ask the children how they know what the person is feeling. Point out the facial features that show the feeling.

If the children remain interested, play a feeling game with them. Show the children the five "feeling faces" and help them identify the feelings expressed. Tell the children you are going to pretend to feel like one of the faces and they should try to guess how you feel. Select one of the plates and place the loop around your neck, turning the face side against your chest so the children cannot see it. Make a face like the one on the plate and invite the children to identify it. Turn the plate around and ask: "Were you right?"

Repeat the procedure, but now have the children take turns doing the choosing and expressing while others continue to guess.

Extension Activity

Have the children draw their own "feeling faces" on plates. Play the game using their creations.

Friendly or Unfriendly... How do Others See Me?

The children develop an understanding of the importance of building friendships by acting friendly toward others.

Activity

The children describe their likes and dislikes about the ways dogs and cats sometimes act. They also describe friendly and unfriendly ways children sometimes act. They increase their understanding of the value of friendships that occur between people as they act friendly toward each other.

Procedures

Ask the children to describe things they like and dislike about the ways dogs and cats sometimes act. As they share their perceptions, focus their attention on friendly characteristics such as: no biting, scratching, or growling; showing affection by licking the face and sitting close, etc. Later ask them to describe things they dislike about the ways other children sometimes act (pushing and shoving, not taking turns, being fussy, saying bad things, calling others bad names, making unfriendly faces, telling lies about others, etc.). They should next describe things they like about the ways other children sometimes act (being kind and polite, taking turns, sharing things, saying nice things, being helpful, making friendly faces, etc.). Lead the chidren to the understanding that the ways they act determine whether others see them as friendly or unfriendly persons. You could ask, "Do you want other children to like you? If so, how should you act so they will like you?" Point out that it is important to have friendships and that friendships can exist only between people who act friendly toward each other.

Extension Activity

Have the children role-play a variety of situations in which both friendly and unfriendly behavior can be demonstrated. For instance:

1. All children waiting patiently in line to receive a special treat (friendly). One child crowding in front of others and not waiting a turn (unfriendly).

2. Four children taking turns sharing three toys (friendly). Four children showing selfishness and not taking turns (unfriendly).

3. Children sitting in a semicircle in front of the teacher without bothering each other (friendly). Children sitting in a semicircle and two children pushing others to have more space (unfriendly).

Ask the children to tell when they feel better about themselves — when they are friendly toward others, or when they are unfriendly toward others?

I'm Growing Up

The children will learn that as they grow up their physical abilities change and develop.

Materials

- Lifelike doll if you are not able to arrange for a six-to-twelve-month-old baby to be present.

Activity

The children identify things they can do that a baby cannot do. They discuss how their abilities improve as they grow up. They then identify things older children can do that they cannot yet do.

Procedures

Introduce the baby to the children. If possible, encourage children to gently touch the baby. You might even allow two or three children to hold the baby on their laps for a few moments. When the introductions are over, discuss the differences between the baby and themselves. You could ask:

How are you different from the baby?

What can you do now that the baby cannot do?

Clarify the children's comments and emphasize the idea that they are growing and changing and also that as they grow their abilities improve.

Follow the same questioning procedure, but this time ask the children to think about older children they know.

Extension Activity

Ask the children to bring from home something they wore when they were babies. Compare these with the clothes they now wear and point out how much they have grown. If there is still interest, ask the children to take the role of babies and act out a simple physical activity such as walking. Then ask them to show how they can now perform the same task.

Open Space for Everyone

The children will learn to identify and express how they feel when in congested areas.

Materials

- Commercially produced flannelboard or one made from cardboard (corrugated recommended) covered with light-blue or off-white flannel material
- Assorted pictures of houses and buildings (trees, grass, plants, and other figures optional); each will have a piece of flannel glued to the reverse side

Activity

The children create an attractive scene on the flannelboard consisting of houses and buildings. They then observe the creation of a highly congested scene. After observing the congested scene and sitting very close together as a group, they share how they feel, or think they would feel, in congested areas.

Procedures

As the other children observe, have two children help you create a scene on the flannelboard consisting of the assorted figures. After the scene is created, ask those who observed to describe what they like or do not like about the scene. Let them take turns adding, taking away, or rearranging the figures to create what they believe is an attractive scene. When each child has had a turn, remove all the figures and create a congested scene of buildings and houses crammed together. Ask them if the scene makes them feel comfortable. You could have them all sit bunched together as a group to illustrate the idea of congestion. Ask them to tell when they feel better: all bunched together, or when they have a choice of space between themselves and others. The purpose is to help them develop an appreciation and need for open space in life situations and for reduction of congested conditions.

Extension Activity

Collect pictures from magazines showing scenes of congested areas and scenes that are well designed with open space. Also collect pictures showing crowds of people and people in areas that are not congested. Have the children separate the pictures into two stacks: congested and noncongested. Ask them to share their feelings about why they prefer or do not prefer to be in congested areas.

Finger-Puppet Talk

The children develop an awareness of actions by others that cause people to experience certain feelings.

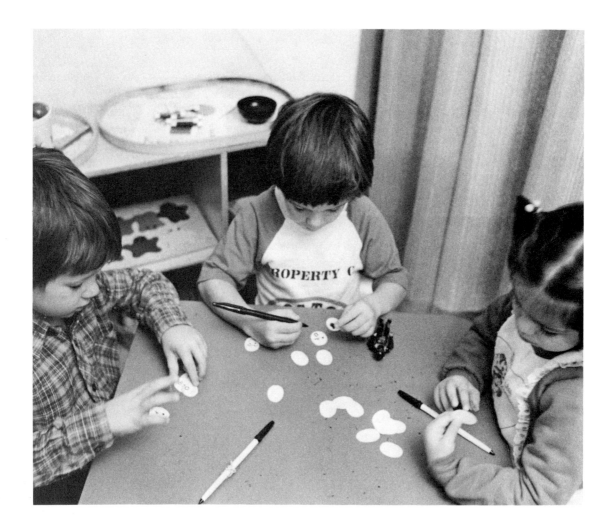

Materials

- Precut, oval-shaped pieces of paper (approximately $1'' \times 1\frac{1}{2}''$)
- Felt-tip pens
- Two-way tape

Activity

The children create finger puppets that suggest a range of emotion. They are then organized into pairs to improvise dialogue with their partners about what made their finger puppets feel as they do. The dialogues are used to stimulate thought about the children's own actions and relationships with others.

Procedures

Give each child several oval pieces of paper and a felt-tip pen. Ask the children to practice drawing faces that suggest very happy, a little happy, a little sad, and very sad feelings. After they practice drawing the four faces, ask each of them to select and then draw one of the four for a finger puppet they will use to talk with other children. When the faces are completed, children should attach them to the first finger of one hand with two-way tape.

Pair the children and ask them to improvise a dialogue with their partners. They are to assume the role of the face they have drawn and explain why they feel the way the face expresses. For instance, dialogue could begin by one child asking the other, "How do you feel?" The other child would give a response consistent with the expression on his or her finger puppet. A next question could be, "What made you feel that way?" A third question could be, "What are some other things that might make you feel that way?" After responses are given to the three questions, the child who asked the questions is now questioned by the other child. Side coaching is a vital role for the teacher throughout the improvised dialogues.

The purpose of the activity is for the children to identify ways people interact and make others feel certain ways. The improvised dialogue procedure is intended to stimulate the children to think about their own actions that can result in others having certain feelings.

Extension Activity

Have two older children or two teachers use hand puppets (or muppets) to create a dialogue that results in happy and/or sad feelings by one or both of them. After the dialogue is completed, involve the children in a discussion about what they believe caused certain feelings between the puppets.

Getting Older

The children will increase their understanding of physical changes that take place in humans and plants as a result of increasing age.

Activity

The children identify significant physical differences between themselves and older people. They develop a better understanding of changes that take place in humans and plants due to advancing age and changes they can expect to experience during the next fifteen years of their lives.

Procedures

Arrange for the children to bring to school the next day on a slip of paper the age of the oldest person living in their homes. Compile the information and prepare a summary showing the range of ages. Have the children identify any special physical characteristics of the oldest person in their homes that are significantly different from the children in the class.

Ask the children if they believe older people can do all the things young people can do. Help them identify some of the ways older people are physically different from young people. Characteristics such as the following could be mentioned and discussed.

Cannot move as fast.

Body is less flexible.

Skin becomes wrinkled.

Spots appear on hands (sometimes arms and faces).

Muscles are not as hard.

Become tired fast.

Eyes become weak.

Hearing loss.

Teeth need to be replaced.

Take the children on a nature walk and help them identify younger and older plants. Particularly help them to find leaves, branches, and/or flowers that are beginning to decay due to advancing age. The purpose of the activity is to help children develop a better awareness of changes that will inevitably take place among humans and plants due to age.

Finally, involve the children in a discussion about some of the changes their bodies will undergo as they get older. It would be advantageous to the discussion if you could arrange for the people of the following approximate ages to be present so the children can make comparisons during the discussion: eight, twelve, sixteen, and twenty-one.

Extension Activity

Invite to your class a very old person who is interested in and willing to talk with your children about how they are different because of age. Discuss with the children prior to the session questions they might ask and ways they can show respect and be polite to the visitor.

Accidents! Oh, Dear!

The children will experience what it is like to do something accidentally. They discover that accidents often cannot be helped and that they happen to everyone.

Materials

- Storybook on the subject of accidents, such as Rosemary Wells's *Unfortunately Harriet* (New York: Dial Press, 1972).
- Accident props: paper cup with a little water in it, sponge, dustpan with small pebbles, paper cup with dried beans, empty milk carton, old magazines, stack of blocks

Activity

The children observe an "accident." They discuss what they saw and consider the fact that accidents happen to everyone and usually can't be helped. They then act out some accidents, using materials provided by the teacher. They discuss the feelings that arise when they do things they don't mean to do and then consider what they might say to someone after that person has had an accident. They then listen to a story about a child who has had an accident.

Procedures

"Accidentally" knock over a paper cup in which you've put a small amount of water. Register surprise ("Oops, an accident!"), and wipe up the water with a sponge. Discuss with the children what accidents are, making the point that accidents happen to everyone and usually can't be helped (that's why they're called *accidents!*). You might tell children how *you* feel when you have an accident.

Have the children act out accidents using the safe materials you provide: dropping a cup of beans, tearing a page in a magazine, spilling the pebbles in a dustpan, knocking over a pile of blocks, dropping a spoon, etc.

Discuss the feelings that arise when people do things they don't mean to do. Ask what the children would say to someone who's had an accident to make the person feel better.

Read them Rosemary Wells's *Unfortunately Harriet*. Discuss what Harriet does to try to fix things. Have them consider why Harriet panics.

Extension Activity

Have the children describe accidents they have had where they hurt themselves. When a child finishes a story, stick a small bandage on or near the spot that was hurt.

Setting Things Right

The children will learn about feelings of anger and how these feelings can be set right.

Materials

- Storybook about quarrels and misunderstandings, such as Charlotte Zolotow's *The Hating Book* (New York: Harper & Row, 1969), *The Quarreling Book* (New York: Harper & Row, 1963), or Rosemary Wells's *Benjamin and Tulip* (New York: Dial Press, 1973).
- "I'm Angry" box constructed from a small box and black wrapping paper
- "I'm OK Now" box constructed from a small box and bright wrapping paper and filled with pennies or dried beans

Activity

The children discuss what it was like to be angry and then have the angry feelings disappear. They then learn to use the "I'm Angry" box, in which they can symbolically place their angry feelings, and the "I'm OK Now" box, in which they place their diffused emotions. They then listen to a story about angry feelings that are set right.

Procedures

Begin by asking the children to think about a time when they were very angry. Then ask them to think about what stopped them from being angry. "Was it a nice thing someone else said?" "Was it a smile and hug from Daddy?" "Was it just time to cool off?"

Show them the "I'm Angry" box. Explain that whenever someone is feeling really angry or unhappy he or she should take a penny from the "I'm OK Now" box and put it in the "I'm Angry" box. Then when they're not angry anymore they can take the penny out of the "I'm Angry" box and put it in the "I'm OK Now" box. Point out that they shouldn't let the angry box stay too full for too long.

Briefly tell the children about the book you're going to read. For example, about *The Quarreling Book* you might say: "This is about a family who has a cranky day, until something quite nice happens to set things right."

Extension Activity

Construct three or four faces on paper plates that show the diffusion of feelings from sadness to happiness, anger to pleasantness, and so on:

Have children act out this progression of feelings.

Are You Afraid?

*The children will develop an awareness of feelings associated with threats to their safety;
they learn to recognize that some fears are based on real things and some are imagined.*

Materials

- Books about fear, such as *Sometimes I'm Afraid*, Jane Werner Watson and Robert E. Switzer (Racine, WI: Golden Press, 1972); *Things I Hate*, Harriet Wittles and Joan Greisman (New York: Behavioral Publications, 1973); *Hello Henry*, Ilse-Margaret Vogel (New York: Parent's Magazine Press, 1965); *The Something*, Natalie Babbit (New York: Farrar, Straus & Giroux, 1970); *There's a Nightmare in My Closet* (New York: Dial Press, 1968) and *You're the Scardy Cat*, Mercer Mayer (New York: Parent's Magazine Press, 1974)
- Magazine pictures (mounted on backing paper) that help illustrate examples of fear

Activity

The children discuss some of the things that frighten them, including things associated with danger and things that are in their minds. They listen to some short stories about children who are frightened and decide whether the danger is real or only in their minds. They then experience in a storybook the real or imagined danger of a child like themselves.

Procedures

Discuss with the children the presence of fear associated with danger. Touch on things they are afraid of such as the dark, storms, other children, being left alone, strangers, loud voices, dogs and other animals, and so on.

Explain that you're going to tell them some short stories about children who are frightened. Ask them to tell you whether the danger is *real* or in the child's mind.

> Tommy is frightened when his brother brings home a puppy. Is this really dangerous?
>
> Milly's mother takes her to school and leaves her with a new teacher. Millie cries. Why is she frightened? Is school really dangerous?
>
> Juan is about to cross the street when he hears a police siren. For a moment he's afraid, so he waits on the sidewalk. Was that the safe thing to do? Is this really dangerous?
>
> Jody sees a stranger in her neighborhood. She is afraid and goes home. Is this dangerous?
>
> William has a doctor's appointment. He is frightened. Is the doctor dangerous? Why is William afraid?
>
> Nancy and Bobby are at the beach. They take a walk. Now they're lost. They're afraid until their daddy finds them. Was this dangerous?

Select one of the books above on real or imagined dangers and read it to the children. Discuss what frightened the characters in the story and what made their fears go away.

Extension Activity

Have the children draw pictures of real or imagined fears. Ask them to tell you about their pictures while you write down their comments. Put their drawings together in a book that they can look at from time to time. Provide time for the children to share their fears with each other.

Food to Make Us Grow

The children will develop an awareness of the importance of diet to good health and that food is important to our health, growth, and energy.

Materials

- Pictures of foods from the main food categories chosen to conform to the story of a child's meals
- Some examples of real foods from the main food categories

Activity

The children are informed about food and nutrition at meal- and snacktimes. They hear a story of what a child ate during the course of a day. They select pictures and real examples of the foods mentioned in the story.

Procedures

Nutrition education cannot be accomplished in one day. Begin informing the children about nutrition at mealtime, snacktime, during food preparation activities, and when feeding classroom pets. Call attention to the main food categories.

1. Bread, cereal products, pastas, seeds: "You need these to run and play." "We need rice and bread so we won't run out of gas." "Cereal gives us energy." "Polly the parrot likes seeds. They keep her feathers shiny."

2. Milk, cheese, yogurt: "Milk makes Molly's bones strong." "The kitties need their milk, just like you do." "This makes your teeth grow. Let's see you smile."

3. Fruits: "Everyone likes fruit. It's sweet." "Oranges make your skin healthy." "I like fruit because it's like dessert." "The guinea pig enjoys apple skins."

4. Vegetables: "These will keep your eyes bright." "The green grass helps our guinea pig grow. It's his salad." "The bunny rabbit likes her lettuce. And no dressing, either!" "Sometimes they're good raw. And sometimes they're good cooked. How do you like your carrots?"

5. Meat, fish, chicken: "We need this for our bones and muscles." "Just a little bit will help us grow strong." "What does your kitty like?"

6. Dried peas and beans: "These are good for growing, too." "We can eat these instead of meat." "These help our muscles grow."

7. Eggs: "These eggs in our pancakes will make them especially good for us." "We can put eggs in our sandwiches instead of ham." "Eggs are good for our bones and teeth."

8. Nuts: "These nuts will make our cookies even better for us." "Let's put a peanut in Polly's cage. It will make her feathers shiny."

Bring together pictures and real examples of foods from these eight food groups. Ask the children to classify them. Very young children may not at first see that, for example, apples and peaches belong in the same group. You might say, "We call these fruits. Fruits taste sweet. Some are crunchy and some are soft. Which one is soft?" The point is that the children begin to see that foods fall into groups and that we should try to eat something from each of these groups every day.

Tell the children a short story about what a child ate during the course of a day. Show them pictures of her meals. You might want to bring to class examples of the real foods she ate.

Sample Story

For breakfast Janey had a piece of papaya, a bowl of oatmeal with honey and raisins, a half piece of toast with apple butter, and a glass of milk.

For snacktime Janey's teacher gave her a piece of orange, a cracker with peanut butter, and a glass of juice.

For lunch Janey ate a bowl of vegetable soup, a tunafish sandwich with lettuce and tomatoes, a raisin-nut cookie that her best friend Tommy's mother sent to school, and a glass of milk.

For dinner Janey's mother made baked chicken, potatoes in their skins, and broccoli; her daddy made his special cucumber and tomato salad. Janey drank a glass of milk. When she was finished, her mom gave her a small dish of ice milk with three strawberries on top.

As you tell the story, have the children pick out the pictures of the things the child ate.

Extension Activity

Ask the children to tell a story about the things they ate one day. Keep a record of their favorite fruits and vegetables and mention these personal favorites at meal- and snacktimes.

The Food and Restaurant Game

The children will learn about foods in the basic food groups through a restaurant game in which they order the foods they like.

Materials

- Plastic or paper plates and forks
- Pictures of various foods mounted on paper from the eight food groups listed in the previous activity
- Aprons for cooks and waiters
- Chef's hat or cap for the cook
- Restaurant corner with one or two tables with chairs, a "stove," pads and pencils for the waiters to take orders

Activity

The children are informed about nutrition and the major food groups at meal- and snacktime. They select pictures of food from magazines that together comprise a balanced diet. Later they play a restaurant game in which customers order foods, waiters take the orders, and cooks fill the orders using food pictures.

Procedures

Inform children about nutrition and the major food groups as described in the previous "Food to Make Us Grow" activity, p. 126.

Help the children select pictures of their favorite meals and foods. Emphasize the need for a balanced menu with foods from each of the food groups. Talk about their choices at meal- and snacktimes.

Set up a section of the classroom as a "restaurant corner." To play the restaurant game, have two children be the waiters, two be the cooks, and two be the customers. Each customer gives an order to the waiter, who then gives the order to the cook. The cooks choose the food pictures that come closest to filling the customer's orders. The waiters then serve the customers. You might want to play the part of a customer yourself. You can suggest more customers as the children get familiar with the ordering routine. In time, the children will extend the game as their imaginations dictate.

Extension Activity

Plan and execute a food-preparation activity that changes the appearance of raw food. For example, make smoothies out of fresh fruit, raisins, and yogurt or applesauce out of fresh apples.

We Need Our Rest

The children will learn to recognize the importance of rest and sleep to good health.

Materials

- Few pictures of people and animals sleeping; include pictures of children and adults
- Storybook about going to bed or the fears of sleeping, such as William Cole's *Frances Face-Maker* (Cleveland, OH: William Collins and World Publishing Co., 1963) or Russell Hoban's *Bedtime for Frances* (New York: Harper & Row, 1960)
- Recording of a lullaby
- Phonograph or piano

Activity

The children look at pictures of animals and people sleeping. They consider the importance of rest for everyone. They listen to a "sleepy" song and act out what animals and people do when they're tired. Later they read a story about going to bed and discuss why some people have a fear of sleeping.

Procedures

Initiate a discussion about rest and sleep by showing the children pictures of animals and people sleeping. Discuss why the people and animals are sleeping, emphasizing the point that everyone needs rest and sleep. Use questions such as: "Why do kitties need their sleep?" "Do big kitties need to sleep?" "How often do people sleep?" "How often do babies sleep?" "Does your mommy need as much sleep as you do? Why?"

Play a "sleepy" song on the phonograph or piano. Invite the children to act out what various people and animals do when they're sleepy. Give each child his or her own person or animal.

Later read to the children stories from one or more of the suggested books about going to sleep. Discuss briefly the fears some have of sleeping, that sometimes everyone fights going to sleep, but that sleep and rest are important for our bodies.

Extension Activity

Keep a rest record for a week by asking each child at the beginning of the school day to tell you when they went to bed and when they woke up. Discuss who woke up first in the morning, who wakes everyone else up, etc. Point out that these things vary from family to family.

The Life Cycle

The students will expand their awareness of the reality of death.

Materials

- Clippers to cut samples of plants
- Plastic bag for collection of samples

Activity

During a nature walk the children collect samples of parts of plants that they later identify as living or dead. Then through telling about pets they have either had or know about that died, they are led into a better understanding of the life cycle of all living things. The children also expand their understanding of the reality of death by telling about relatives and friends of their families who have died.

Procedures

Take the children on a nature walk. Guide them to collect samples of both living and dead parts of plants that can be taken to the classroom (small branches, leaves, stems, flowers, blossoms, fruit, bark, etc.). After returning to the classroom, have the children separate from the collected samples those that appear to be dead. Point out in a discussion that some plants live only a short time, whereas others (such as great trees) may live for hundreds of years. It is important to point out that all plants eventually die.

Ask the children if they have ever had pets or know about a friend's pet that died. Also inquire if they know how old the pet was when it died and what made it die (accident, lack of care, old age, etc.). Guide the discussion to help the children understand that all living things have life cycles, including humans. When appropriate, permit the discussion to include identification of relatives and friends of their families who have died and causes for their deaths (accident, illness, old age, etc.). It is important that the discussion not overwhelm the children with a fear of death but rather that it present death as a reality that we all need to acknowledge as an eventual part of the life cycle.

Extension Activity

Ask the children to talk with their parents about ways they can help pets live longer. Conduct a discussion the following day during which the children have an opportunity to share what they have learned from their parents. Point out the importance of proper food, treatment of illness, observance of safety precautions, protection from the elements, vaccinations, etc., as all important to the prolongation of the lives of animals and humans.

Feelings Game

The children will learn that people sometimes show their feelings.

Activity

As a group, the children role-play several feelings that are named. They then listen to the reading of brief situations and take turns role-playing the specific feelings described. They learn to show the feelings that people sometimes have.

Procedures

Name several feelings and ask the children as a group to role-play each. For instance, you might say "lost and scared," and children role-play the feeling. Then "sad because your toy is broken," "happy after receiving a nice birthday gift," "angry because someone took your favorite book," "lonely because you are at home by yourself," "hurt because you bruised your knee," etc.

After the children role-play feelings as a group, have them take turns role-playing the following situations. Read each situation twice, then select a child to role-play the scene.

> Wanda looks everywhere for her blue socks. She looks in drawers, under the bed, in the toy box. After looking for a long time, she becomes very sad and feels like crying because she cannot find her blue socks.
>
> Bobby works fast to help his father. He picks up the tools, puts them in a box, sweeps the floor, then takes a quick bath. He feels very happy because his father is taking him to see a movie.
>
> Rosa feels sleepy. She falls asleep and later wakes up. She looks around and sees the older girl from next door. The girl is to stay with her while her parents are away. Rosa feels so lonely.
>
> Robin is sleeping. He wakes when he hears some strange noises. He looks around the room but can't see what is making the noises. He begins to feel scared.
>
> Kevin has just learned that his favorite uncle is coming to pick him up and take him to the park. He quickly gets dressed, combs his hair, and becomes very excited when his uncle arrives.

Point out in a final discussion how people sometimes show their feelings about things and sometimes hide their feelings.

Extension Activity

Have the children act out a feeling one at a time. Those watching should guess what the feeling is, then verify it with the child who was acting. After the feeling is identified, another child could make up a story about why the actor felt a certain way.

Nursery Rhymes Express Feelings Too!

The children will learn to recognize that rhymes are one way people express their feelings about things.

Activity

The children name and tell about rhymes they have heard or know. Four rhymes are then presented to help the children learn to recognize the messages they communicate. The activity is concluded with an explanation of different ways people express their feelings, rhymes being one of the ways.

Procedures

Ask the children to name as many rhymes as they can. As each rhyme is named, ask if they can tell what the rhyme is about. Explain that rhymes, songs, stories, poems, etc., all express how people feel about certain things.

Read one of the following rhymes several times. Let the children who can memorize fast say the rhyme with you as they are ready. Explain the meaning of the words that may be unfamiliar to the children. Then, when they have had sufficient experience with one of the rhymes, ask them to share what they believe are the important ideas and/or feelings expressed. Follow a similar procedure for each of the four rhymes. Suggested ideas and feelings are included after each rhyme.

Cock-Crow

Cocks crow in the morn
  To tell us to rise,
And he who lies late
  Will never be wise;
For early to bed
  And early to rise,
Is the way to be healthy
  And wealthy and wise.

(Proper rest and sleep will make our bodies healthy and our minds active and alert.)

Bedtime

The Man in the Moon looked
  out of the moon,
Looked out of the moon
  and said,
" 'Tis time for all children
  on the earth
To think about going to bed!"

(The Man in the Moon encourages children to go to bed and get the sleep they need to stay healthy.)

Little Pussy

I like little Pussy,
  Her coat is so warm,
And if I don't hurt her
  She'll do me no harm;
So I'll not pull her tail,
  Nor drive her away,
But Pussy and I
  Very gently will play.

(Being kind and playing gently with Pussy will result in her being a cuddly friend that will not scratch or bite.)

Ding, Dong, Bell

Ding, dong, bell,
  Pussy's in the well!
Who put her in?
  Little Tommy Lin.

Who pulled her out?
  Little Johnny Stout.
What a naughty boy was that,
  To try to drown poor pussy-cat.
Who never did him any harm,
  But killed mice in his father's barn.

(A naughty, mean boy put the pussy-cat in the well and tried to drown her, even though the pussy had never done any harm to the naughty boy. But a good boy pulled Pussy out of the well and saved her.)

Near the end of the activity explain that feelings about things can be expressed by our facial expressions, by the gestures we make with our bodies, by the general way we act, by the words we speak, by the songs we sing, and by the words we write. Explain that a rhyme is a method of writing about the ways we feel.

Extension Activity

Help the children make up a rhyme about a subject of their choosing that expresses the way they feel about something. After they memorize the rhyme, ask them to say it for their parents and explain the feelings expressed in it.

Angry Feelings? What Do You Say?

The children will learn to express in words the angry feelings they have.

Materials

- Two hand puppets

Activity

The children are given an imaginary situation and act out angry feelings using hand puppets. They then discuss words and phrases that help diffuse anger.

Procedures

Give two children hand puppets. Present them with a situation that calls for an expression of anger, annoyance, or irritation. For example, you might say, "You are playing with your tea set and Jose comes and takes away all the cups. What do you say?" Ask the children to dramatize the situation using the hand puppets. Guide them to use verbal rather than physical expressions of anger. Use verbal cues to prolong the dialogue to a conclusion satisfying to both sides. For example, you might say and ask, "How do you feel? What do you say when you're angry? Yes, I can tell you're angry from your voice. If Jose gives it back, what do you say?"

Discuss together the phrases that help defuse angry situations, such as "Excuse me," "I'm sorry I hurt you," "Can I help?" "Please don't," "It's all right."

Extension Activity

Have the children discuss behaviors that make angry situations worse, such as hitting, biting, yelling, and so forth.

Why Are Bugs Scary?

The children will learn to recognize why they fear some insects.

Materials

- Live specimens or pictures of insects children are likely to encounter in your area, such as house or garden spiders, ground roaches, ants, termites, grasshoppers, etc.
- Clear plastic jars or plastic drinking glasses
- Lids or cellophane wrapping paper
- Rubber bands to fix wrapping paper on glasses
- Two shallow boxes or trays
- Two six-inch circles cut out of yellow construction paper, one showing a happy face, one showing a scared face
- Paste or glue

Activity

The children take turns grouping the insects according to whether they are afraid of them. They talk about their reasons for being afraid and listen to the feelings of others. They then discuss which insects are important to avoid.

Procedures

If you are using live specimens, secure their containers' lids or use plastic wrap so children can handle the containers. Paste a happy face on one box and a scared face on the other one.

Ask the children to take turns dividing the bugs into two groups: bugs that scare them and bugs that don't. Have them group the insects in the appropriate box according to their feelings. They should then try to explain why the bugs in one box are scary and the ones in the other are not. Guide with questions, pointing out how not everyone is equally scared.

Help the children learn to identify reasons they are afraid, such as fear of the looks or touch of insects, fear of being stung, and influence of others. Encourage children who are not afraid of harmless insects to discuss why bugs don't frighten them.

Discuss which bugs are important to avoid, such as bees, wasps, some spiders, red ants, and so forth.

Extension Activity

Keep a collection of insects in the classroom where the children can observe them. You might later want to ask children whether they have changed their feelings about some of them.

What Can You See Without Your Eyes Game

The children will learn that the sense of touch and smell can help them discover new properties of ordinary objects.

Materials

- Strips of cloth for blindfolds
- Assortment of small articles children encounter frequently, such as block, orange, lemon, rubber ball, puzzle piece, drinking cup, bottle cap, carrot, bar of soap, comb, washcloth, etc.
- Box or container to hold items

Activity

The children begin by discussing how a person who cannot see is able to identify something, such as chocolate cookies baking in the oven. They play a game in which they identify common objects using senses other than sight.

Procedures

Discuss how some people cannot see with their eyes. Ask how a person who cannot see would know that there were chocolate chip cookies baking in the oven. (He or she would smell them.) Guide children toward the idea that people can see with their ears, noses, fingers, toes, and so forth.

Tell the children they will play a game in which they will try to guess what something is without seeing it. Blindfold two or three volunteers and hand each a different object from the box. Encourage the children to use other senses. (If the object is safely edible, include taste as well as touch and smell.) After the children say what the objects are, the others can say whether they are correct.

For variety you might have the blindfolded volunteers find objects you name from among the others in the box. This affords the children the opportunity to handle several objects before making a choice.

Extension Activity

Invite someone with impaired vision to talk briefly to the children about seeing without eyes, or blindfold a volunteer and ask another child to lead him or her around the room. Discuss how the experience felt.

I Show My Feelings with My Body

The children will learn that they often express their inner emotions through their bodies.

Materials

- Large white sheet to use as a shadow screen
- Line or rope
- Clothespins
- Slide projector or light source
- Weights to keep sheet stationary

Activity

The children observe a demonstration of anger expressed in body language. They identify the emotion and explain how they recognized it. Volunteers act out their feelings through body movement. The children then take turns acting out basic emotions behind a light screen.

Procedures

Keeping your face away from the children, demonstrate anger through body movement, such as stamping your foot and shaking your fist. Ask the children whether they can identify how you're feeling. Discuss how they can recognize anger. Guide them to see that your body is expressing your feelings.

Invite two or three volunteers to demonstrate a feeling through body movements. Help them become aware that we express many feelings through our bodies, just like dancers, without talking or making faces.

Have the children go one by one behind the shadow screen. On your signal, they should act out a feeling that can be expressed through the body without facial expressions: surprise, anger, fear, pain, happiness, being lost, tiredness, etc. You might say "happy," and the child will show this feeling with hands, legs, and body movement. Encourage the children to be original. The children watching are to try to identify the feelings being expressed.

Extension Activity

Play music that expresses emotions, such as "Peter and the Wolf." Ask one or two children to act out the feelings behind the screen. The others try to identify the feelings expressed.

How Do We Show We're Sad?

The children will identify sad feelings and learn that these feelings can change.

Materials

- Photograph, drawing, or picture from a magazine showing a child in a situation evoking sadness, such as saying goodbye to a friend or losing a favorite toy (see master no. 4 in the appendix)

Activity

The children respond to a picture showing a sad situation. They take turns demonstrating how they express feelings of sadness. They discuss different ways people can help make a sad person happy again.

Procedures

Show the children the picture. Encourage responses with questions such as the following.

What is happening here?

How is the person feeling? How can you tell?

What will she do now? Do you think he will cry?

What can we do to make her feel better?

Ask one or two volunteers to demonstrate how they show feelings of sadness. Have the other children take turns role-playing different things to do to make the "sad" person happy, such as a warm hug, pat on the back, playing with the person, etc.

Extension Activity

The children draw or paint either a happy picture or a sad picture. Ask them to tell you why the person in the picture is sad or happy, and what made the person that way.

Caring for Pets

The children will learn that pets need food, shelter, medical care, and love from their owners.

Inside the photo, on the poster:

Always be kind to animals,
Morning, noon, and night;
For animals have feelings too,
And furthermore,
    they bite.

Materials

- Pictures and/or photographs of pets, which children bring to school
- One or two school animals (guinea pig, bird, mouse, etc.)

Activity

The children bring to school photographs or pictures of real or imaginary pets. Using a classroom pet as an example, they are led in a discussion about animal care. The children are then invited to share personal stories about their real or imaginary pets.

Procedures

Ask the children to bring photographs of their pets to school. Children without pets can bring a picture of an animal they would like to own.

Initiate a discussion on the handling and care of animals. Use the classroom pet as a focus, demonstrating the proper way to care for it and handle it. Some questions to guide discussion are the following.

How do we keep our pets happy?

What do pets need to live?

Who feeds the pets?

What happens when kitty gets sick?

What do they like to eat?

Do our pets need love? How do we show love?

How do our pets like to be touched?

Should all pets be handled the same way?

Invite the children to share pictures of their real or imaginary pets. Have others ask questions of the owners. Elicit responses that animals depend on their owners for food, shelter, medical care, and love.

Extension Activity

Invite a representative from the local chapter of the Society for the Prevention of Cruelty to Animals to talk with the children about animal care, or arrange a visit to the agency offices in your area.

The Time Cycle

The children expand their understanding of personal needs that are met during each twenty-four hour period.

Activity

The children identify the kinds of things they do during a typical twenty-four-hour period and learn to recognize how these activities relate to meeting personal needs. They expand their understanding of why it is important to meet these needs. The children then pantomime needs as they are named, explaining how their bodies are affected if the needs are not met.

Procedures

Ask the children to share with you the kinds of things they do from one day to the next (go to school, eat, sleep, play, watch television, help with things at home). Lead them to discover how the kinds of things they do are related to meeting their personal needs — learning, relaxing, sleeping, satisfying hunger, exercising, helping with chores that contribute to the good of others, maintaining good hygiene. You might ask questions such as these to stimulate thought about their personal needs.

Do you need to sleep every night? Why?

Do you need to eat several times a day, or only once? Why?

Do you need to learn how to do things such as read? Why?

Do you need to exercise your body? Why?

Do you need to do things to help other people? Why?

Do you sometimes need to rest? Why?

Point out that a day and night (twenty-four hours) represents a period of time during which we all participate in a continuing cycle of events concerned with meeting our personal needs.

For a summary activity you could have the children pantomime meeting each of the needs you name (sleep, eat, exercise, etc.) and then share how their bodies are affected (emotionally and physically) if they fail to meet the needs.

Extension Activity

For those children you believe are ready, make a clock with hands the children can move and help them learn to tell time. A game could eventually be played in which a personal need is named and a child moves the hands of the clock to indicate a general time when that particular need is met during a twenty-four-hour cycle of events.

We Help when Others Are Ill

The children will learn to recognize a need to assume "helping responsibilities" when others become ill.

Activity

The children describe ways other family members have helped when a member of the family became ill. Hypothetical situations are then staged to increase the children's awareness of the value of assuming responsibilities to help those who become ill. They also role-play a helping scene for an older member of the family who cannot walk.

Procedures

Ask the children to tell about members of their families who have been — or may currently be — ill. Without probing to learn the kinds of illnesses, encourage the children to describe ways members of the family help those who are ill (preparing special food, being as quiet as possible, getting things for them, helping them walk, washing them, helping them get dressed, etc.). If the children have difficulty identifying ways others help an ill person, you might use a doll to stage a hypothetical illness and have the children help you provide care for the doll. You could also describe a hypothetical situation in which a father is ill and has to remain in bed for a long time. The children would then describe ways they can help to comfort and care for him as well as tend to many of the chores he would normally do. The goal is to expand the children's understanding of the need for others to assume "helping responsibilities" when people become ill.

If appropriate for the age level, you could have the children role-play a situation in which a doctor, nurse, and members of the family provide care and help for a grandparent who is unable to walk. Encourage the children to share what they could do to help.

Extension Activity

For follow-up activities, have the children periodically share experiences they have had at home when family members became ill. Ask them to tell about ways others helped, and describe things they did to help.

When You Get Sick at School

The children will learn how to alert their school caregivers when they don't feel well.

Materials

- Hand puppet

Activity

The teacher uses a hand puppet to initiate a discussion with the children about illness symptoms. They learn where and when to report how they feel to adults.

Procedures

Use the hand puppet to initiate a discussion on signs of illness. You might say:

Hello. This is Teddy and he doesn't feel too well today. When he woke up this morning he felt tired, but he went to school anyway. Now his nose is runny and his forehead feels warm. What should Teddy do? What is wrong with him? Have you ever felt like this? What did *you* do?

Invite the children to ask the puppet questions on his "symptoms" and feelings. Encourage talk about similar personal experiences. Guide the discussion toward the idea that the children should notify their teacher when they don't feel well.

Use the opportunity to explain classroom and school procedures regarding illness.

Extension Activity

Invite the children to role-play with you the procedures to follow when they are ill or hurt. You might ask a child to pretend he or she is sick, while you take the role of the concerned teacher. Elicit the child's description of feelings by asking questions such as, "Where does it hurt?", "Can you show me?", and "When did it start hurting?"

CHAPTER 6

Decision-Making and Problem-Solving Activities

Share and Tell ... What to Bring?

The children will develop an awareness of the need to consider many related factors before making decisions.

Activity

The children participate in a discussion aimed at helping them examine alternatives prior to deciding what to bring from home for a share-and-tell day. After considering related factors, they make decisions about what to bring and then confirm their decisions with their teacher and parents.

Procedures

Schedule with the children a share-and-tell day. They are each to bring something from home they will show and tell the other children about.

Involve the children in a decision-making process that will help them become aware of possible items they could bring and items they should not bring. The following factors could be discussed to help them examine alternatives prior to making decisions.

Ease of portability to and from school.

Size of item in terms of handling by young children.

Storage in school before and after showing.

Sturdiness or delicateness; danger to item in transporting.

School rules regarding bringing certain items to school.

Needed care for item during the day (such as pets).

Anticipated interest in item by other children.

Knowledge about item that can be shared with others.

Item that parents will agree they may bring.

Cost of item; security within the classroom.

The purpose here is to encourage the children to examine as many alternatives as possible before deciding what they should bring. Help them arrive at decisions they will then discuss with you and with their parents. Should some children have to change their decisions for any reason, the changes should be discussed with all the children in terms of factors they might have overlooked in examining alternatives.

Extension Activity

Help the children examine alternatives before deciding where they would like to go on a field trip. Factors such as length of time required, costs, location, availability of restrooms, interest to most children, difficulty in making arrangements, approval by parents and the school, and benefits to children from the trip should be considered before making a decision.

Group Decisions Are Fun!

The children will learn to participate in a group decision-making process.

Materials

- Looseleaf book (either commerically produced or homemade)
- Crayons
- Paper

Activity

The children develop a class book that includes samples of their best work. They use criteria identified by the teacher to make a group decision about which items to include and select a cover design for the book.

Procedures

Suggest to the children they develop a class book during the school year that includes samples of their best work. The book could include drawings, pictures they have colored, examples of handwriting and lettering, and other things of interest to them and appropriate for inclusion. Explain that they will use a group decision-making process to determine which items should be included in the collection. As activities are completed and one or more items are selected for the book, name several criteria related to the activity they should use to decide which to include. Guide them to make a group decision using the criteria. Point out during the process the need to listen to the views of others and the value in making a decision as a group. Encourage a positive attitude toward the group decision-making process.

Ask each student to use two colors to create a possible design for the cover of their book. When the designs are completed, have them decide as a group which design they will use for the cover.

Extension Activity

Make available materials for each child to create an individual looseleaf book in which they will include what they consider to be their best work during the year. Encourage them to use the criteria you identify to decide what to include. Each child should create a two-color design for the cover of the book. Toward the end of the year, provide time for the children to share their books with each other. Also display them for view during a parents' night.

Decision Making ...with Help

The children will learn the value of gathering information and considering alternatives before making decisions.

Materials

- Catalogs of school equipment and/or printed brochures

Activity

The children are asked to participate in a decision-making process concerned with the purchase of a new piece of equipment for the school. They are guided to gather information, consider alternatives, and make a decision, which they present as a recommendation. Relationships are then drawn between the decision-making process they experienced and other life activities requiring decisions.

Procedures

Identify a piece of equipment of interest to the children that your school is about to buy (wagon, rhythm instrument set, jumbo Tinker Toy set, etc.). Catalogs and/or other printed information showing the equipment should be available for you to show the children. Explain that you want help in solving the problem of, for instance, which wagon to buy. Show the pictures of different wagons. Ask the children to suggest things they should consider in making a decision (size, color, sturdiness, general attractiveness of design, type of wheels for surface on which it will be used, cost, ease in use by small people, length of time for delivery, etc.). After they have gathered the information needed and considered alternatives, have them make a decision that they will present as a recommendation to the person responsible for making the purchase.

Point out that good decisions can be made only after gathering information and considering all related matters. Relate the information-gathering and consideration of alternatives process to other life activities familiar to the children that require decisions (which store to go to, which toy to buy, what games to play at a birthday party, etc.).

Extension Activity

Prepare a brief letter to parents explaining that you are helping children learn to gather information and consider alternatives before they make decisions. Include a brief response sheet on which the parents will include three things they consider are most important when deciding on which car to buy. Tally the returned responses. Read all the responses to the children, naming the three mentioned most. Point out how parents also gather information and consider alternatives before making decisions.

Let's Grow a Garden

The children will learn how to gather information and consider alternatives before making decisions.

Activity

The children participate in a decision-making process relative to beginning a miniature garden. After gathering information concerning what will grow in the designated garden area, they consider alternatives and decide what to plant and where to obtain the items needed to begin the garden.

Procedures

Invite the children to help you devise a plan for a miniature garden. The garden should be outdoors if weather conditions are acceptable and space is available. Flowerpots or other containers could be used as a substitute. After concluding where the garden will be located, involve the children in a decision-making process relative to what they will grow.

Explain that before deciding what to grow they should collect information. They could ask their parents, neighbors, or others to learn what plants (food-bearing, ornamental) might grow in the selected area. When you feel that sufficient information has been gathered, explain all the alternatives available to them and have them decide as a group what they will grow in their garden.

Next involve the children in learning what they will need to begin their miniature garden. This could be another information-gathering process to learn who might donate seeds, seedlings, cuttings, soil, containers, tools, etc. When sufficient information has been gathered, designate a day when all the items will be assembled and planting will begin. (See the "Planting, Growing, Tending, and Sharing" activity p. 56, for beginning the garden.) The goal of this activity is to help the children learn how to: (1) identify a problem that needs a solution, (2) consider sources of information relevant to finding a solution, (3) identify alternative solutions, and (4) make a decision based on valid data.

Extension Activity

Involve the children in a similar decision-making process to plan a class library. Questions concerning where it will be located, what kinds of books or magazines it will include, how large it will be, rules for its operation, identification of who might make donations to it, and others could all be included in the decision-making process. Again stress the need to identify alternatives and make decisions based on the best information available.

Safe-Unsafe Safari

The children will develop a better awareness of safe and unsafe areas and conditions in their school.

Activity

The children share their perceptions of safe and unsafe areas of their school and areas that are made unsafe when rules are not observed. They then go on a "safari" to observe all areas and confirm and/or change their original perceptions. After the safari, they share their perceptions and discuss the value of children and adults becoming more aware of the need for safe conditions.

Procedures

Ask the children to name areas of the school they believe are unsafe for small children. Then ask them to name areas they believe can become unsafe due to failure to follow rules. As much as possible through discussion, have the children describe from memory areas of the school in terms of safe and unsafe conditions.

Take the children on a safari for a closer look at all areas of the school. Pause at each and ask the children to describe both safe and unsafe conditions they see, and how failure to follow rules could result in an area that looks safe becoming unsafe. They should look specifically for: areas where steps are irregular in height, playground equipment and doors where fingers can be pinched, railings that may not be strong enough to support the weight of bodies, dark areas where lighting is not sufficient, storage areas where items are stacked and could fall, tool rooms that should be restricted areas, etc.

After the safari, discuss with the children their observations. Help them decide if their perceptions prior to the safari changed afterwards. Conclude the discussion with a sharing of ideas about why both adults and children should develop an awareness of safe and unsafe conditions where they attend school, where they live, and where they spend their leisure time.

Extension Activity

Plan with the children for them to report the next day on three unsafe areas (or areas that could become unsafe) where they live. Ask them to look carefully to confirm their opinions, then report to the class on what they observed. Invite the children to share their findings and discuss why we all need to become more aware of such conditions.

Stop-and-Go Decisions

The children will learn the value of safety procedures for crossing the street and consider the consequences of their decisions and actions.

Materials

- Red, green, yellow, and black construction paper
- Cardboard backing sheets, approximately 10″ × 20″
- Masking tape or chalk
- Glue or scissors

Activity

The children discuss the meaning of green, yellow, and red traffic signals, and they are introduced to basic street-crossing safety rules. They play the roles of traffic lights and pedestrians and discuss their behaviors. They then apply decision-making skills to traffic situations.

Procedures

Prepare a set of traffic lights showing the "stop," "caution," and "go" signals by gluing colored circles onto backing sheets as shown here.

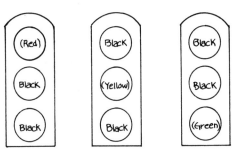

Use masking tape or chalk to draw on the floor a typical intersection showing pedestrian crossings. Your layout should be large enough for the children to practice crossing the street.

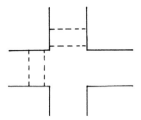

Discuss with the children what each of the signals means. Share safety rules such as:

Always look first before crossing, even if the light is green.

Always look behind you before stepping off the sidewalk.

The yellow light that follows the green light means stop.

Have one child take the role of a traffic signal and two or three the roles of pedestrians. Have the children take turns acting out the safe way to cross the street. To get the game started, you might first take the part of traffic signal and model how to change signals by holding up different sheets. Ask other children to judge the performance of the actors. Guide with questions such as, "Did Peter stop and look first?" and "Did Mary wait for the light to change?"

Involve the children in addressing the questions and situations shown here. For each one, hold up the appropriate light.

The signal is red, but there are no cars. What do you do? (Stop, don't cross.)

The signal is green. You run across without looking. (No; you always look first, then cross without running.)

You are on the sidewalk and the light turns yellow. Do you run across quickly before it turns red? (No, you wait — yellow means stop.)

The signal is red, but there no cars. Your friend says, "Let's run across." What do you say? (No; wait for the green light.)

Extension Activity

Take the children on a walk to a nearby traffic light to observe street-crossing behaviors. The children discuss what they see, considering the appropriateness and safety of pedestrian behaviors.

Places I Want to Visit

The children identify places they would like to visit and the articles they should take to accommodate their personal needs.

Materials

- Old suitcases small enough for a child to carry, airline flight bags, beach bags, purses, shopping bags, etc.
- Variety of clothes for different purposes such as sweaters, jackets, swimsuits, dress-up clothes, play clothes
- Other articles suitable for packing such as shoes, change purses, bath soap, empty food cartons, picnic items, beach towels, toys, socks

Activity

The children first discuss the places they would like to visit and then name some of the things they would need to take with them. They take turns selecting a special place and packing a bag of articles appropriate to that place. They then share the contents of their bags and suitcases and tell why they chose certain items.

Procedures

Place the materials you have collected in an area where the children will have easy access to them. Ask the children to name some of their favorite places to visit both near and far away such as the beach, grocery store, another city, church, or their grandparents' house. Discuss what sorts of things they would need to pack to take with them when visiting their favorite place. For example, when they go to the beach they would need swimsuits, towels, beach toys, and maybe something to eat.

Have the children take turns packing a bag with the things they would need to take to their favorite place. When they are finished packing, have them share the contents of their bags with the group. Ask them to explain why they chose certain items.

Extension Activity

Play a game in which the children examine the contents of various bags that you have specially prepared and try to guess where the person who packed that bag is going. For example, you could prepare a beach bag, briefcase, suitcase packed with warm clothing, shopping bag, and so forth.

CHAPTER 7

Values of Learning Activities

Learning Skills Are Important

The children identify skills essential to learning.

Activity

The children identify learning as one of their school activities. They become aware of why learning activities and the development of learning skills are important.

Procedures

Ask the children to name the school activities they participate in such as playing, eating, resting, learning, going on excursions, doing art work, singing, and playing games. Discuss with them why learning activities are important and why all children need to develop learning skills.

The following suggestions are provided for illustrating the learning skills they need to develop.

Listening   Have the children stand and quietly respond to your spoken directions such as "tip-toe," "sit down," "put hands behind head," and "pat your tummy." Explain the importance of listening skills.

Observing   The children could observe your actions and describe one by one what they see. You might: (1) clap your hands once, touch your knees, jump once; (2) rub your tummy, turn around, sit down; (3) take three hops, pat your head twice, snap your fingers; or do other kinds of actions that can be observed. Explain the importance of observation skills.

Thinking   Present several problems such as the following, and ask the children to help you solve them by describing what they think would be good solutions.

Problem 1: The playground equipment needs to be cleaned. What will be needed to clean the equipment, and how should they organize to do the job?

Problem 2: There is too much noise by children during nap times and rest times. What can be done to reduce the amount of noise?

Problem 3: Some children do not eat all their lunch. What could be done to get children to eat all the food and prevent wastefulness?

Explain the importance of thinking skills to learning.

Remembering   Make a short statement and ask students to repeat in unison the statement you made. Ask three children to do specific things (move blocks or books to new locations, interview parents to learn the cities where they were born, find out how old their brothers and sisters — or best friends — are, etc.). After they have completed their responses to your directions, ask them to state (remember) what you originally asked them to do. Explain the importance of remembering skills.

Other learning skills such as organizing information and following directions could also be included in the procedures.

Extension Activity

Ask the children to interview parents or others to find out what they believe are things children should do to be successful in learning activities. The children should take turns sharing what they find out. Point out during this activity how: (1) listening was important to learn what parents or others said, (2) remembering was important to later recalling what was said, and (3) thinking was important to organizing their thoughts to report what was said.

Telling the News

The children will learn that "news" describes the activities people engage in and that people are interested in the news.

Materials

- A newspaper

Activity

The children discuss what news broadcasters do. They look at a newspaper and have pointed out to them some items of interest. At sharing time they tell news items about events that happened in school and at home.

Procedures

Ask the children whether they or their parents watch the news on TV. Discuss what news broadcasters do, if necessary explaining that they tell people what's happening in their communities and the world. Show the children a newspaper. Ask them to explain what a newspaper is for. Point out items that may be of interest to them, such as movie announcements, food sales, toy advertisements, news items involving children, and photographs.

For several days, or as a regular activity, have the children do a news broadcast during sharing time. Ask the children to recount interesting events about classroom happenings such as the following.

Susie's daddy took her to the zoo last Saturday.

John finished three puzzles today.

Yesterday, Tommy went to the dentist.

Maria has a new red dress today.

Yesterday we had spaghetti for lunch.

Ms. Brown's slippers got lost today, but she found them in the sandbox.

Encourage them to fill in details by asking who, what, where, when, and how questions. What is important is that they see that some events are of interest to everyone.

Extension Activity

Ask the children to bring in news from the neighborhood for news-sharing time. Ask who, what, where, when, and how questions to draw out the details.

Setting Goals for Myself

The children will learn the value of goal setting to self-improvement.

Materials

- Index card for each child in your group

Activity

The children are helped to master a specific skill. It is later explained that mastery of the skill was a goal set by the teacher for all the children in the group. The children are then guided to set goals for themselves, which they work toward accomplishing. As goals are reached, dates of completion are recorded and new goals set.

Procedures

Identify a specific skill that you have been trying to help all the children develop (saying the alphabet, printing certain letters of the alphabet, saying days of the week or the twelve months, writing or saying numbers, etc.). Continue to work at the skill until all the children have mastered it. Then explain that you set a goal for your group, the goal that all children in the group would be able to demonstrate the skill you named. Point out that goals are used by everybody to identify what it is they want to be able to do and that once a goal is set, they work to accomplish the goal.

Prepare an index card for each child in your group. Each child is to identify a goal he or she wants to accomplish within the next few weeks. Help them identify goals that relate directly to the learning activities (intellectual and/or physical) you have planned. As they accomplish the goals, write the dates of completion on the cards, and then help each child set a new goal. Emphasize the value to self-improvement of being goal oriented and building a positive self-concept.

Extension Activity

In a letter to parents, explain the procedures you have used to help the children set and then work toward accomplishing goals. Encourage parents to help their children set goals related to home life that can be accomplished in a few weeks. As these goals are realized, have the children share in class what their goals were, their experiences in accomplishing them, and the feeling they had after reaching the goals.

Imagination ...Understanding Myself

The children will learn to expand their use of imagination.

Materials

- Box measuring approximately 8 " × 8 " × 8 ", without markings

Activity

The children's curiosity is aroused as they are shown an empty, closed box. The teacher gives clues about what could be in the box, then asks questions to stimulate thought. After sufficient answers are elicited, new clues are given and the game continues. The goal is to help the children use given clues as a basis for creative thought.

Procedures

Creativity is defined as a process of combining known factors into new relationships to create something new — a new product, a new way of thinking, a new way of doing something. The purpose of these procedures is to stimulate creative thought and help the children learn to recognize that they have creative potential.

Hold the box in your lap. Begin looking at it in an interesting and inquisitive way to arouse curiosity. Tell the children you will give them some clues and that they are supposed to use the clues (known factors) and imagine what is in the box. The first clues are: "It has soft fur, it does not eat food, it does not make sounds." Use prompter questions such as the following to stimulate thought. "Is it an animal?" "Is it alive?" "Where can it be found?" "Is it sold in a store?" "Is it small enough to fit in this box?" (Stuffed animal toy, or other appropriate answer.)

For another round, tell them the item in the box is soft, round, and is not alive. Questions such as the following could be used to stimulate thought: "Is it something to eat?" "Is it used only at a playground?" "Is it a toy?" "Will it fit into this box?" "Is it something parents use, or do only children use it?" (Toy balloon, ball, or other appropriate answer.)

Continue the game using other clues as long as interest is evident. You could have some children take turns holding the box and giving clues. They will be using their imaginations as they make up clues.

For a final round, place an interesting object in the box, give clues, ask prompter questions, listen to other suggestions, then show what you have placed in the box. Tell about the item if it is unfamiliar to them.

Extension Activity

Invite the children to make up very short stories about a new toy that is the best in the world they could have. Encourage them to tell what it looks like, how it feels, ways they can play with it, how big it is, what color it is, why they like it, etc. Ask them questions that will help to stretch their imaginations.

Your Ears Can Help You Learn

The children will become more aware that listening carefully can help them learn.

Materials

- Pictures or drawings mounted on index cards showing objects whose sounds the children can imitate — car, drum, rain, clock, dog, cat, etc. (see master no. 5 in the appendix)

Activity

The children imitate the sounds of various things and others guess what they are. They then discuss how the ability to hear relates to successful participation in many kinds of activities.

Procedures

Point to your ears and ask the children what they are for. Guide them to see that their ears tell them about the world just as their eyes, mouths, and hands do.

Ask how they would react if they were crossing the street and heard a car horn. Discuss other sounds that tell them about something: the wind in the trees, sound of rain, a dog barking in a neighbor's yard, a baby crying, etc.

Play a sound-imitation game. Show a child one of the pictures and have him or her imitate the sound associated with it. You might have the other children try to guess the object imitated before you reveal the picture. After the children guess correctly, invite them to imitate the object together.

Help them see that their sense of hearing helped them guess what the object was. Also emphasize how the ability to hear is related to success in learning, enjoyment during play, and safety.

Extension Activity

Ask the children to close their eyes and be absolutely silent for a few moments. Ask them to listen for sounds they don't normally hear when they are busy working and playing. Have them try to identify what they think are making the sounds.

Looking and Remembering Game

The children will learn to value the development of looking and remembering skills.

Materials

- Assorted items (marble, empty thread spool, beanbag, alphabet block, Tinker Toy, scissors, felt-tip pen, large button, small ball, paperweight, etc.)

Activity

The children play a game in which they are shown six items arranged in a certain order. The items are then put in a box, given to the first player, and the player has to "beat the clock" by placing them in order within a given period of time. Other combinations of six items are shown to other players as they participate in the game. The number of items shown gradually increases. The children later discuss how learning to look and remember relates to learning in all areas.

Procedures

Explain that a game will be played in which a player may look at six items arranged in a line on a table or on the floor for ten seconds (use a timer!). The items are then removed and placed in a box. The box is given to the player; the player removes the items from the box and has ten seconds to arrange them in the order seen earlier. The challenge is to look quickly and remember what is seen. The order and combination of items is changed for each new player. The leader, of course, must recall the order of the items for each new player.

When all the children have had an opportunity to play the game, discuss with them how looking and remembering skills are important to learning in all areas (developing physical skills others have; learning to make things, use tools, cook, participate in sports; etc.). Invite them to verbalize some of the ways they believe learning to look and learning to remember will help them in the future.

After discussion, play the game again, challenging the children by gradually increasing the number of items arranged in a certain order.

Extension Activity

Play another looking and remembering game with a different set of twenty assorted items. When the children can name all twenty, put them in a box, then quickly remove any five and place them on the table or floor (no order is needed). After five seconds put them back in the box. The child selected for the first round is then to name the items seen. The game continues as each child views a different combination of five of the twenty items. Gradually increase the number of items shown to six, seven, eight, nine, etc.

Goals: Step 1, Step 2, Step 3 ...

The children will learn that goals often have to be accomplished in steps or stages.

Materials

- Red stars
- Gold stars
- Index cards

Activity

The children work at a skill until they master it. At various points in the process they are shown by stars that they are developing a skill in steps. After they have mastered the skill, they discuss their accomplishments. The children then identify another goal to accomplish and are kept informed of their progress.

Procedures

Identify a specific skill or procedure you would like the children in your group to master. This should be one that is fairly complex and will have to be accomplished in more than two steps or stages. For example, being able to climb to the top of the jungle gym alone may require these steps:

1. Climb to the first rungs without fear.
2. Climb to the second level with confidence.
3. Climb to the top.

The children are to work at the skill until they have mastered it. Prepare a card for each child on which you record the stages of their progress and award them a red star for each accomplished step. When they achieve the final goal, date it and attach a gold star. Discuss with the children how their goals were accomplished — not all at once, but in steps. Show them their cards and review their progress over time. Or, you may want to keep them informed of their progress as they work toward achieving their final goal.

Prepare another index card for each child. Help each one identify a goal to accomplish that is related to the learning activities you have planned. As they work toward accomplishing the goal, note with red stars the achievement of subgoals. You might also date each step and record any important details at each stage. Keep the children informed of their progress. When the final goal is reached, award the gold star. Throughout the activity emphasize the value of being goal oriented.

Extension Activity

Invite the children to talk about their achievements, the stages and steps involved, and how they felt as they were working to achieve their final goal. You might then want to extend the final goal to a further one. For example, if a child has mastered a difficult puzzle, you could help select a more challenging one.

More on Learning Skills

The children will learn to use questioning skills that are necessary to learning.

Materials

- Apple
- Block
- Crayon
- Paper bag

Activity

To learn how to ask questions, the children will play a game in which they try to guess the contents of a paper bag, using questions that elicit a "yes" or "no" answer. After playing the game, they discuss how questions help people learn.

Procedures

Put the items in the bag and seal it. Tell the children you have something in the bag and if they are curious and ask lots of questions they can find out what it is. Explain that they cannot touch or look in it but must guess what is in the bag. Guide them toward the idea that they can ask questions and you will answer either "yes" or "no." Point out that they should listen carefully to the questions and answers. You might give them a hint of the bag's contents: "This is something good to eat" "Is it red?" "Is it round?"

Provide clues and hints so as not to prolong the activity unnecessarily. If interest prevails, repeat the procedure with the other objects.

Discuss with the children how asking questions helped them guess. Have them consider some of these questions:

What kind of question does your mother ask when she cannot find the newspaper?

What kind of question does your daddy ask when he wants to know what you did in school?

What does your sister ask when she wants a new toy?

What kinds of questions do you ask when you meet someone for the first time?

Lead them to the idea that questions are helpful. You might take the opportunity to ask each child a question that seeks information: "What's your favorite food?" "Who lives next door?" "What do you like to do after school?"

Extension Activity

Play the question guessing game with other objects so that children begin to learn how to converge on an answer. Keep objects and procedures simple. For example, you might tell them you have a crayon in the bag, then have them converge on the right color by process of elimination. Or you could tell them you have fruit in the bag, but they can ask only about its shape and color: "Is it red?" "Is it round?"

Things I Use in School Game

The children will learn to classify objects according to the educational uses they serve in school.

Materials

- Assortment of school materials familiar to the children, such as:

paintbrush	measuring spoons
eraser	measuring cups
pencil	plates
blocks	paperclips
drawing paper	notebook
book	felt-tip pens
paint	crayons
two or three musical instruments	paste
yarn	magnifying glass
backing sheet for stitchery	puzzle
beads	insect specimen
string	scissors
record	spool

Activity

After practicing simple classifications of assorted school materials, the children play a game in which they select two materials and describe how they are used and why they go together.

Procedures

Spread the objects on a table and discuss them with the children. Have them spend a few minutes classifying the objects according to color, shape, and size. Guide them toward the idea that all are materials used in school to help them learn. Ask the children to tell you what they have used some of the objects for.

To start them off, pick up two objects and say, "These go together because I can write my name on the paper with this pencil." Invite one of the children to choose two objects and say how they go together. The two objects are then placed in front of the child. The next child repeats the process.

Continue the activity until no more uses can be expressed or when the children have gone through the entire assortment. Discuss the experience, pointing out that school materials can be used in many ways to help children learn.

Extension Activity

Discuss with the children the school materials older brothers and sisters use. Bring some of these to class to show the children. Include textbooks with interesting pictures, binders, pencils, ball-point pens, maps, rulers, and so forth. Let the children speculate on their uses. You might want to demonstrate the uses of rulers, protractors, and compasses. If appropriate, let the chidren experiment with some of these.

Places We Learn

The children will develop an interest in learning new things during visits to different places.

Materials

- Collection of pictures cut from magazines that show specific locations such as school, home, church or temple, park, store, gas station, factory

Activity

The children select from a collection pictures of places where they believe they could learn new things. They then share the kinds of things they believe they could learn. They also share experiences at different times during the year to tell about other places they have visited and the things they learned during their visits.

Procedures

Show the pictures to the children. Ask them to select a picture of a place where they believe they could learn something new. If they select the picture of a store, for instance, ask them to share what they believe are the kinds of things they could see and learn during a visit to a store (range of products available, how products are displayed to be attractive, how store is organized to provide service, etc.). Follow a similar approach for each picture they select. The goal is to help the children develop natural interest in learning something new during visits to different places.

Periodically during the year have sharing sessions to provide the children opportunities to tell about places they have visited and things they learned during their visits. Encourage inquisitiveness and curiosity as ways to learn new things during visits to new places.

Extension Activity

Take the children on an excursion to a place of business near your school. Explain that you will not tell about the place they are going. They are to look during the visit to learn as much as they can from what they see. After returning to the school, involve them in a discussion designed to reveal what they have learned. Questions such as the following could be used to prompt sharing.

What were the people doing?

Did any of the people wear uniforms?

Were the people selling things?

Did the people look busy?

Did it look like a happy place?

What kind of equipment (machines) did you see?

Were services being provided to customers?

First I Do It, then It's Your Turn

The children will learn to lead while others follow, and follow while others lead.

Activity

The children watch the teacher lead a simple clapping rhythm and then echo the rhythm back. After they get the idea of following what the leader does, the children take turns being leaders. When they finish, they discuss what leaders have to do and what followers have to do.

Procedures

Tell the children that you are the leader and they are the followers. Perform a simple clapping rhythm and ask them to echo it back by clapping the same pattern. Repeat the procedure until they get the pattern right. Try two or three variations so they get the idea of echoing what you've done. Repeat each variation until they get it right.

Ask the children, "Who will be our next clapping leader?" Name a new leader, explaining that everyone who wants to will get a turn. Guide the children to keep their rhythms simple so others can follow. The leaders will repeat the same rhythms until followers get them right.

Discuss the activity, guiding the children to discover that followers had to look and listen carefully and that leaders had to keep the rhythms simple so others could follow.

Some simple rhythm patterns are:

___ ___ ___ ___
___ ___ ___ PAUSE

__ __ __ __ ___ ___

___ __ __ ___ __ __

Extension Activity

Substitute any behavior that can be copied to play the game again (slapping thighs, beating a drum, moving the hands and fingers, etc.). Help the children learn to observe and listen carefully before they begin echoing the patterns of the leader.

CHAPTER 8

Awareness of the World of Work Activities

Guess Who I Am?

The children will learn to identify activities associated with various jobs.

Materials

- Index cards with pictures or drawings of workers doing their jobs

Activity

The children pantomime the actions of various workers then guess who the workers are.

Procedures

Collect pictures of workers and activities the children will recognize, such as a truck driver driving a truck, a police officer directing traffic, and a nurse taking a child's temperature. Show the children one of the pictures and ask them to name the worker and the activity. Have them pantomime the activity together.

Pass out cards with pictures and ask the children to keep their cards hidden from others. Have the children take turns pantomiming the work activity while the others try to guess who the workers are.

Extension Activity

Read work-related stories to the children. Good resources are:

Elsa Beskow's *Pelle's New Suit*, (New York: Harper and Brothers, 1929)

Virginia Lee Burton's *Mike Mulligan and His Steam Shovel*, (Boston: Houghton Mifflin, 1939)

H.A. Rey's *Curious George Takes a Job*, (Boston: Houghton Mifflin, 1947)

Workers' Tools Game

The children will expand their understanding of the world of work and the tools and equipment needed to do certain kinds of work.

Materials

- Pictures of tools and equipment (see master no. 6 in the appendix)

Activity

The children learn to name some of the tools or equipment certain workers need to do their work. Then, in two groups, they play a game in which the groups take turns naming the workers that correspond to the pictures of implements shown to them. The group with the highest number of points wins the game.

Procedures

In a brief discussion, ask the children to name some of the tools and/or equipment the following workers need to do their work.

ice-cream vendor (ice-cream cart or truck)

firefighter (water hose)

lifeguard (life preserver)

When the children understand the procedure, divide them into two equal groups and have them play a game. Show one picture and give the first group a chance to name the worker. If they correctly name the worker, give the group one point. If they do not correctly name the worker, the second group will have a chance. After a group correctly names the corresponding worker for a picture, the other group then has a turn. The group with the most points wins the game. Help the children gain a better understanding of the implements needed to do certain kinds of work and skills needed in the use of the implements.

Master no. 6 shows the following tools and equipment:

gasoline pump (gas station attendant)	car jack (auto repair person)
violin (musician)	hoe (farmer)
cash register (store clerk, salesperson)	cement trowel (mason)
helicopter (pilot, repair person)	chair and tooth drill (dentist)
tractor (construction worker)	stethoscope (doctor)
mail truck (postal worker)	computer (computer operator)
stove (cook)	side of beef and saw (butcher)
boards, hammer, nails (carpenter)	typewriter (typist, secretary)

Extension Activity

Play another game in which two groups of children name the corresponding sport for the following items, which you could obtain pictures of or draw on the chalkboard.

football helmet (football)	hurdle (track and field)
basketball hoop (basketball)	volleyball (volleyball)
tennis racket (tennis)	bow (archery)
golf clubs (golf)	gloves (boxing)
bat (baseball)	rod and reel (fishing)
hockey stick (hockey)	

Work Sounds

The children will learn to recognize sounds of some work activities.

Materials

• Index cards with pictures of familiar work situations

Activity

The children create sounds associated with many different work situations.

Procedures

Collect pictures of workers in situations having sounds children will recognize, such as a road worker with a drill, an ambulance driver in an ambulance, and a tree trimmer with a saw. Show the children one of the pictures and ask them to make the sounds they "hear" in the picture.

Pass out cards with pictures and invite children to take turns pantomiming the activities and imitating the sounds they hear in the pictures. Have others try to guess what the workers do.

Extension Activity

Take the children on a walk during which they look and listen for and then identify worker sounds. Later have them name the kinds of work they identified and imitate the sounds they heard.

Working Hard

The children will learn the value of working hard, of being confident in one's abilities, and of being willing to help when help is needed.

Materials

- Pictures cut from magazines and mounted on sturdy paper showing people of all ages working at different jobs. Include pictures of people doing physical labor.
- "Chore box" the size of a shoebox
- Small pieces of colored paper

Activity

The children look at pictures of people in various work situations and tell stories about them. They discuss the chores they do at home. They consider various tasks that need doing around the classroom; these are written on paper and put into a "chore box." At an appropriate time, the children pick chores out of the box and complete them together.

Procedures

Show the pictures to the children and ask that they tell stories about them. If necessary, guide the children with questions: "What's the little girl doing? Is her brother helping too?" "What is this woman doing with the computer?"

Briefly discuss the chores the children do at home and school. Compare their chores, for example: "Tanya feeds the animals and Benjamin helps put the clothes away."

Have the children think of small chores around the classroom that they could complete during a short chore period. These should be tasks apart from the routine tasks they do in class, such as putting things away when they are finished. Write down the chores on slips of paper and put them in the chore box. At an appropriate time, let the children pick out chores from the box and do them together during a short chore period.

Extension Activity

Read to the children from a storybook about working such as *Katy and the Big Snow*, Virginia Lee Burton (Boston: Houghton Mifflin, 1943) or *Friday Night is Papa Night*, Ruth A. Sonneborn (Viking Press, 1970). Stress the way Katy fulfills her responsibilities and how hard Papa works yet how happy the children are to see him. You might use these stories as opportunities to talk about what the children's parents do for a living. Point out that everyone works, but avoid being moralistic about this.

People Have Feelings ... Even about Work

The children will learn to better recognize the feelings they have and some of the feelings adults have about the work they do.

Activity

The children discuss feelings they sometimes have and the causes for their feelings. They listen to adults talk about things they like and dislike about the kinds of work they do and the feelings they have toward their work. An intended outgrowth of the activity is that the children develop a better awareness of their own feelings.

Procedures

Involve the children in a discussion about ways they sometimes feel. Have them name some of the things that make them feel certain ways, such as angry, happy, lonely, afraid, and sad. Use their responses to introduce the subject of feelings people have toward the work they do.

Arrange for at least five adults (parents, friends, others) who have jobs to visit your class at different times to talk about the kind of work they do. They should first tell about aspects of their work that will be of interest to the children, then describe things they like and dislike about their work. Ask them to describe specific feelings they have about the things they like and dislike. The purpose is to acquaint children with the range of feelings people often have toward the kinds of work they do, but that they are able to function successfully in fulfilling their work responsibilities. Emphasize during the procedures the importance of becoming aware of the feelings we all have toward various activities.

Extension Activity

Schedule a work hour during which each child in your group is responsible for completing work that will help to improve the school environment. When the work hour is completed, ask the children to tell whether they liked or disliked the kind of work assigned and the feelings they had while completing the work. Again, the goal is to help them become aware of the feelings they have toward activities in life.

Worker Shadowing

The children will develop a greater appreciation for workers and the kinds of work they do.

Activity

The children visit places of work and "shadow" individual workers as they do their jobs. They later discuss their observations to gain a better understanding of the kinds of skills and physical strength required to do certain jobs and the attitudes of workers toward what they do.

Procedures

Arrange for an excursion during which the children will visit several workplaces of interest to them (fire station, factory, warehouse, computer center, technical school, newspaper offices, etc.). At each location arrange for a spokesperson to explain briefly (at the child's level) what some of the workers they are to see will be doing. Then as they observe individual workers, ask the children to look closely at the skill(s) the worker demonstrates and listen carefully as he or she describes the work being done. The goal is for the children to "shadow" a worker for a brief period as actual work is being done. There will be advantages in visiting places where the children's parents work.

After the excursion, and on another day, ask the children to share their interests in the kinds of work they observed. "What kind of work interested you most?" "Did the workers seem to enjoy the work they were doing, or did they look unhappy?" "Which jobs required a lot of strength?" "Which jobs required a lot of thinking?" These questions and others could be used to rekindle their interest and help them focus on specific things they observed.

Extension Activity

Ask the children to imagine what kind of work is done by workers in an ice-cream or candy factory. After they have shared their imagined jobs, take them on an excursion to the place discussed and let them shadow some of the workers. Following the excursion have them compare the kind of work they imagined with what they actually observed.

What Am I Doing?

The children will learn to identify familiar work activities.

Materials

- Pictures or drawings of familiar work activities mounted on index cards
- Box to hold cards (optional)

Activities

The children take turns pantomiming familiar activities, and others guess what they are.

Procedures

Select work activities familiar to the children such as cooking a meal, checking out groceries, washing dishes, weeding a garden, rocking a baby, mowing the lawn, emptying the garbage, driving a car, and sweeping the floor.

The children take turns picking a card from the box and pantomiming the activity pictured. Each child should keep the picture hidden from the others while acting. Give the children time to adequately portray the activity. Encourage them to use their bodies and voices to help the others identify what they are portraying. Ask the children to withhold their guesses until each pantomime is completed.

Extension Activity

Set up a play area to include these activities: a grocery store with a toy cash register, a kitchen with cooking utensils, a doll corner, etc. Provide opportunities for the children to engage in imaginative work-play in these areas.

Who Helps Us Clean Up?

The children will learn about what the school custodian does and how they can help.

Materials

- Custodial utensils such as bucket, mop, broom, dustpan, vacuum cleaner, soap

Activity

The children listen to the custodian tell about his or her job. They learn about the utensils used in cleaning work and how these help the custodian do the job. The children then explore simple rules they can observe to help the school custodian.

Procedures

Arrange for the school custodian to visit the children and share what he or she does every day. Ask the worker to bring some utensils to show the children. You might suggest that cleaning solutions be brought so that the children can be cautioned about them, or you can provide the materials and utensils you want the children to learn about.

If possible, allow the children to handle the cleaning utensils such as the broom and vacuum cleaner. The children might enjoy actually seeing a demonstration of some custodial tasks.

Later, discuss together the things the children can do to help make the custodian's job easier. Compile a list of helpful rules, for example:

Wipe up spills.

Do not litter.

Remove toys from sandbox and put them away.

Keep socks in cubbyholes.

Turn off faucets in bathrooms.

Extension Activity

Help the children compose a thank-you note to the school custodian. If children can write their names, have them sign the note individually.

Why Do We Use the Telephone?

The children will develop an awareness of reasons we use the telephone.

Materials

- Two toy telephones

Activity

With the teacher, the child assumes an adult role and engages in a dialogue on the telephone. They talk about why people use the telephone. They exchange roles, with the child initiating the conversation.

Procedures

Ask a child to choose a role such as doctor, nurse, grocery store clerk, or taxi driver. Take the part of a caller and initiate a dialogue with the child appropriate to that role such as making an appointment, calling for a prescription, ordering groceries, or arranging to be picked up at your address. Responding to the child's conversation, help create a meaningful dialogue.

Briefly discuss why people use the telephone; for example, to make appointments, talk to a good friend, and invite someone to play.

Ask the child to telephone someone he or she would like to talk to and say that you will pretend to be that person. Have the child dial a number and initiate the conversation. Encourage an interesting dialogue by varying your voice and tone, asking questions, and prompting.

When the procedures are understood, pair the children and have them take turns participating in conversations.

Extension Activity

Have the children name all the rules they can think of to ensure good telephone etiquette. Make a list; remind them of the rules they suggested during other telephone dialogue activities.

Living Together ... Working Together

The children will develop an awareness of the need for a spirit of community.

Activity

The children learn about a community project that is being conducted and identify a specific way they can contribute to it. They visit a site for some phase of the project. They also learn to recognize the value of people in a community working together to accomplish a common goal.

Procedures

At a time during the year when an appropriate community project is being conducted, help the children learn about ways mutual concerns and cooperation by community groups can contribute to the good of all. Select a project such as a paper-recycling campaign by a charitable organization, a fund drive to repair an important public facility, or volunteer work to aid a senior citizen program that the children can contribute to in some way. Explain in terms the children can understand *what* the project is intended to accomplish, *why* there is a need for people to work together in the project, *how* individuals and groups such as schools can help with projects, and the good such a project can bring to the community in general. It is recommended that an excursion be planned to take the children to a site where some phase of the selected project is being conducted (site where improvement is to be made, collection center, senior citizen center, etc.). The goal of the activity is to impress upon the children the need for a spirit of community, that when those who live together also work together cooperatively we all receive benefits.

Extension Activity

Have your class (or school, if appropriate) identify a small-scale project they could conduct to improve some aspect of their school life. Help them determine what needs to be done, why they are doing it, how they should proceed to do it, and the good they will derive from their efforts. Name a specific completion date for the project.

Our Neighborhood Changes

The children will develop an awareness that neighborhoods grow and change.

Materials

- Play materials similar to those found at a construction site: trucks, bulldozers, shovels, buckets, tools, wooden blocks for building, etc.
- Camera and film

Activity

The children visit a neighborhood site that is undergoing change. They discuss the experience and use toy props to dramatize their understandings. They are provided space and materials to simulate what they learned on the excursion. They continue to visit the neighborhood site to witness changes occurring over a period of time.

Procedures

Check out the community around your school for an area that is undergoing change: a new house or subdivision, road construction, urban renewal, or any construction site that will illustrate the concept of neighborhood changes. Take the children on a field trip to observe the work and activity occurring there. Note together the materials that help bring about change (truck, shovels, nails, tools, bricks, etc.). Take pictures of the site for future discussion.

Discuss the trip with the children, eliciting the idea that neighborhoods grow and change over time. Provide play materials for the children to act out their understandings as they discuss what they observed on the trip.

Over the next few days, provide materials, space, and opportunities for the children to simulate the activities they observed. You might keep the play area unstructured or, if you prefer, provide buildings made of blocks, which the children then change.

If future trips to the site are possible, plan them over time so the children can see how the project progresses. Take pictures and display them in the classroom, where they can be discussed.

Extension Activity

Read the children a story about change such as Virginia Lee Burton's *The Little House* (Boston: Houghton Mifflin, 1942). Discuss the changes mentioned in the story.

What Will I Be Doing?

The children will expand their awareness of the value of learning to the world of work.

Materials

• Assorted pictures of adults in work situations

Activity

The children share imagined job roles (if any) they will have when they become adults. They then learn about general job types in which adults work and the value of learning activities in school to successful work in their adult years.

Procedures

Display assorted pictures of adults in work situations. Then ask the children if they have ever imagined what kind of work they will be doing when they become adults. Invite them to share their fantasies by naming the kinds of jobs they thought they might do. Keep a list of the jobs they name and use prompter questions to help them think of other jobs.

The *Occupational Outlook Handbook* published by the U.S. Department of Labor Statistics provides these occupational cluster headings:

industrial production	scientific and technical
office	mechanics and repairers
service	health
education	social science
sales	social service
construction	performing arts, design, and
transportation	communications

For each of the above clusters, discuss job types that the children might understand. The goal here is to expand their awareness of the world of work. Point out that most of the years of their lives will be spent working at a job and that developing skills in preparation for work begins at a very young age. You might conclude the discussion by explaining how children's daily learning activities help them develop skills needed for each of the job clusters (learning to follow instructions, learning to read and write, developing physical skills, developing social skills, making good decisions, becoming aware of personal needs and skills, etc.).

Extension Activity

Have the children interview their parents about the value they place on learning at an early age in preparation for the world of work. A very short response questionnaire could be designed, sent home with the children, and returned the next day. Share with the children what their parents' views are concerning the value of learning while young and the advantages early learning brings in later years.

Appendix

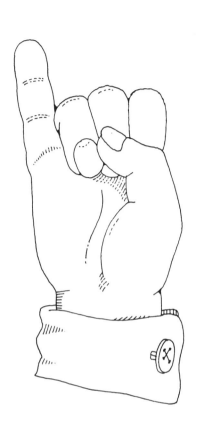

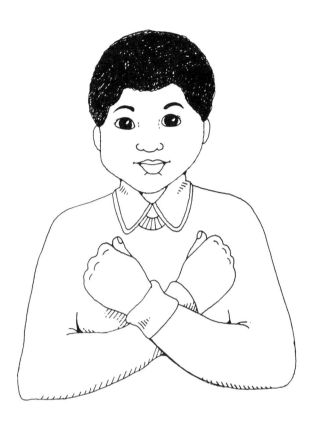

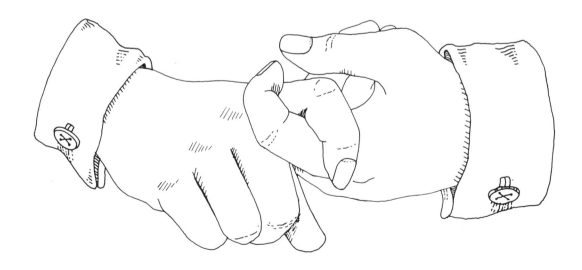

Relationships with Others (see p. 92) 225

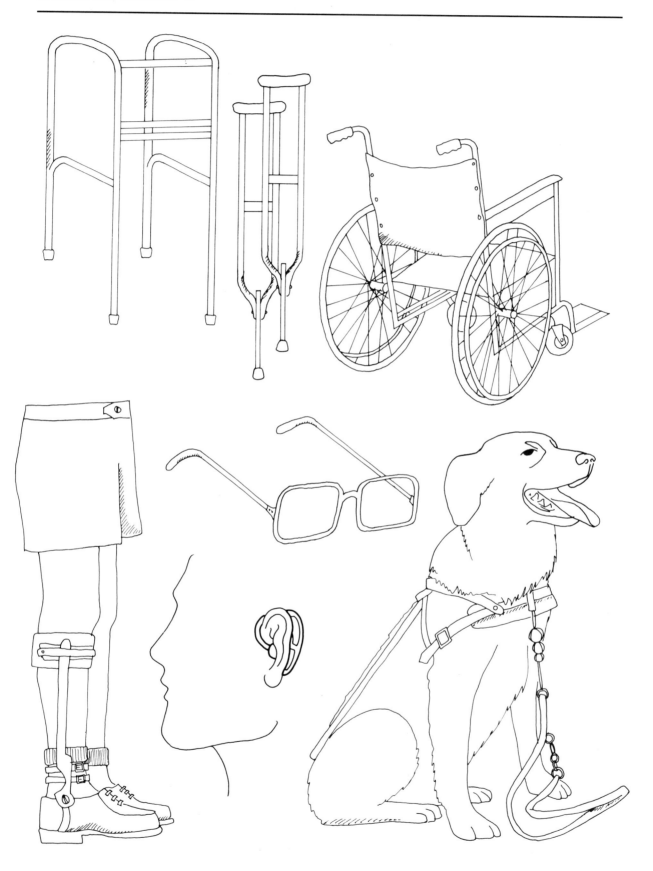

Awareness of the World of Work (see p. 200)   *231*

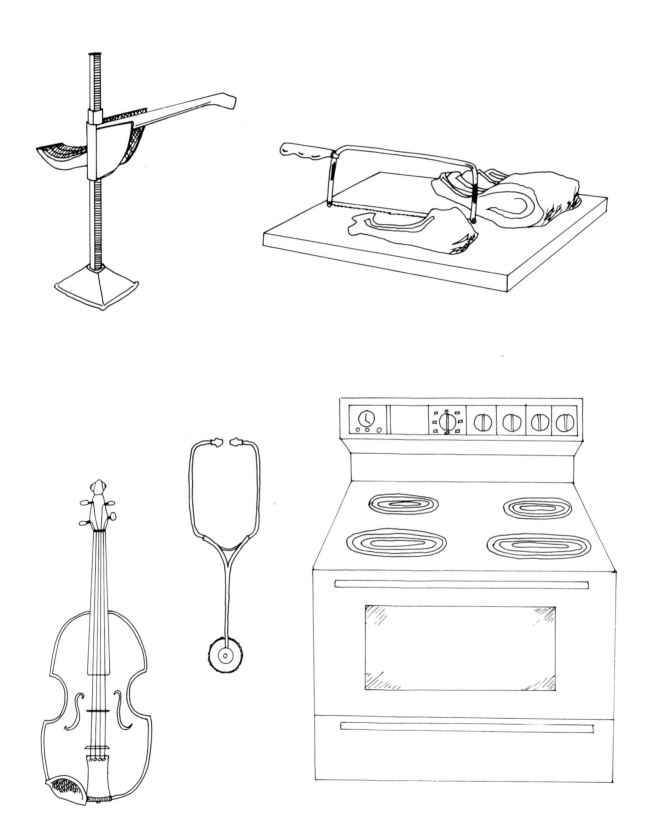

Awareness of the World of Work (see p. 200) 233

Index of Behaviors for Six Categories of Activities

	Page	Self-Awareness and Understanding	Relationships with Others	Physical and Emotional Growth	Decision Making and Problem Solving	Values of Learning	Awareness of World of Work
● primary emphasis ○ secondary emphasis							
Self-Awareness and Understanding (Chapter 2)							
Develop awareness of ways people are alike and different from each other.	10	●	○				
Identify own interests and interests of others.	12	●	○				
Compete with self to improve abilities.	14	●					
Identify and accept physical characteristics.	16	●		○			
Interact with others and imitate patterns.	18	●	○				
Learn that feelings are natural and okay.	20	●		○			
Identify and develop awareness of the five senses.	22	●		○			
Learn the value of self-assessment and improving the school environment.	24	●	○				
Learn that names have unique rhythms.	26	●					
Learn that voices have unique sounds.	28	●					
Learn the names of body parts.	30	●					
Become sensitive to actions and feelings of family members.	32	●	○				
Learn that likes and dislikes for foods may be imagined.	34	●		○			
Learn uniqueness of one's own skin color and shades of skin.	36	●		○			
Learn that individuals have unique physical attributes and qualities.	38	●	○	○			
Relationships with Others (Chapters 3 and 4)							
Contribute ingredients to a soup and learn to cooperate with others.	42		●				

	Page	Self-Awareness and Understanding	Relationships with Others	Physical and Emotional Growth	Decision Making and Problem Solving	Values of Learning	Awareness of World of Work
Develop positive attitudes toward awareness of problems of physically handicapped persons.	88		●				
Build positive attitudes toward equal opportunities for men and women.	90		●				
Develop appreciation for and knowledge of sign language as a communication tool.	92		●				
Develop positive attitudes toward cultural differences.	94		●				
Learn that people form opinions about others by observing behavior.	96		●				
Recognize that objects are made to help disabled persons overcome handicaps.	98		●				
Develop awareness of differences among cultural groups.	100		●				
Learn that families are of different sizes, and explain the broad definition of *family*.	102	○	●				
Become aware that there are many career choices and that one's sex does not determine choice.	104		●				○

Physical and Emotional Health (Chapter 5)

	Page	Self-Awareness and Understanding	Relationships with Others	Physical and Emotional Growth	Decision Making and Problem Solving	Values of Learning	Awareness of World of Work
Become aware of feelings and accepting them.	108	○		●			
Develop understanding of importance of building friendships and acting friendly.	110	○	○	●			
Learn that physical abilities change and develop.	112	○		●			
Identify and express feelings caused by congested situations.	114	○		●			
Develop awareness of actions that affect others' feelings.	116	○	○	●			
Increase understanding of changes in humans and plants resulting from advancing age.	118	○		●			
Learn that everybody has accidents.	120	○		●			
Learn about feelings of anger and how they can be set right.	122	○		●			

	Page	Self-Awareness and Understanding	Relationships with Others	Physical and Emotional Growth	Decision Making and Problem Solving	Values of Learning	Awareness of World of Work
Develop awareness of threats to safety; recognize some fears as real, some imagined.	124	○		●			
Develop awareness of importance of diet to good health, growth, and energy.	126			●			
Learn about basic food groups.	128			●			
Recognize importance of rest and sleep to good health.	130			●			
Expand awareness of the reality of death.	132	○		●			
Learn that people sometimes show their feelings.	134	○		●			
Recognize that rhymes are ways people can express feelings.	136	○		●			
Use words to express feelings of anger.	138	○		●			
Recognize why some people fear insects.	140	○		●			
Learn that the sense of touch and smell can help in discovering properties of objects.	142	○		●			
Learn that feelings are often expressed through the body.	144	○		●			
Identify sad feelings and learn that they can be changed.	146	○		●			
Learn about the needs of animals.	148			●			
Expand understanding of personal needs during each twenty-four hour period.	150	○		●			
Recognize a need to help when others are ill.	152			●			
Learn how to alert caregivers when feeling ill.	154		○	●			
Decision Making and Problem Solving (Chapter 6)							
Develop an awareness of the need to consider related factors before making decisions.	158				○		
Participate in a group decision-making process.	160		○		○		
Learn value of gathering information and considering alternatives before making decisions.	162				○		

238

	Page	Self-Awareness and Understanding	Relationships with Others	Physical and Emotional Growth	Decision Making and Problem Solving	Values of Learning	Awareness of World of Work
Gather information and consider alternatives before making decisions.	164				○		
Develop awareness of safe and unsafe areas in the school.	166			●	○		
Value safety procedures for crossing the street, and consider consequences of decisions.	168				○		
Identify places to visit and articles to take to meet personal needs.	170	○			○		

Values of Learning (Chapter 7)

	Page	Self-Awareness and Understanding	Relationships with Others	Physical and Emotional Growth	Decision Making and Problem Solving	Values of Learning	Awareness of World of Work
Identify skills essential to learning.	174	○				●	
Learn that "news" describes activities of people, that people are interested in news.	176					●	
Learn the value of goal setting to self-improvement.	178	○				●	
Expand use of imagination.	180					●	
Become aware that listening carefully can help learning.	182					●	
Learn to value the development of looking and remembering skills.	184					●	
Learn that goals are accomplished in steps or stages.	186					●	
Use questioning skills to aid learning.	188					●	
Classify objects according to educational uses they serve.	190					●	
Develop interest in learning new things during visits to various places.	192					●	
Lead while others follow; follow while others lead.	194		○			●	

Awareness of the World of Work (Chapter 8)

	Page	Self-Awareness and Understanding	Relationships with Others	Physical and Emotional Growth	Decision Making and Problem Solving	Values of Learning	Awareness of World of Work
Identify activities associated with various jobs.	198						●
Expand understanding of the world of work and tools and equipment needed to do work.	200						●

	Page	Self-Awareness and Understanding	Relationships with Others	Physical and Emotional Growth	Decision Making and Problem Solving	Values of Learning	Awareness of World of Work
Recognize sounds of work activities.	202						●
Value working hard; show confidence in personal ability and willingness to help others.	204	○	○				●
Recognize personal feelings and feelings adults have about the work they do.	206	○					●
Develop appreciation for workers and work they do.	208						●
Identify familiar work activities.	210						●
Learn about school custodial work and how to help.	212						●
Develop awareness of reasons we use the telephone.	214		○				●
Develop awareness of the need for a spirit of community.	216		○				●
Develop awareness that neighborhoods change and grow.	218		○				●
Expand awareness of the value of learning to the world of work.	220		○			○	●